TABLE OF CONTENTS

*On the Lord's Day I was in the Spirit,
and I heard behind me a loud voice like a trumpet (1:10).*

—— 1 ——

*In the Spirit
on the Lord's Day*

Revelation 1–5

DIMENSION ONE:
WHAT DOES THE BIBLE SAY?

Answer these questions by reading Revelation 1

1. To whom did God give the revelation? (1:1a)

2. Why was the revelation given? (1:1a)

3. How did God make known this revelation given to Jesus
   Christ? (1:1b)

4. How is John described? (1:2)

5. What must those who are blessed do with John's account? (1:3)

6. Who is John's message for? (1:4a, 11)

7. Who is described as the one "who is, and who was, and who is to come"? (1:4b, 8)

8. Who else is the message from? (1:4b-5a)

9. How is Christ described? (1:5a)

10. How does John describe himself and his audience? (1:5b-6)

11. What does John say about Jesus Christ being seen again by the world? (1:7)

12. Who is speaking in 1:8?

13. How does John describe himself with reference to the members of the seven churches? (1:9)

14. Why was John on Patmos? (1:9)

15. As John describes his experience of being in the Spirit on the Lord's Day, what is he told to do? (1:11)

16. What are the first things John sees in his vision? (1:12-13)

17. What are the symbolic items of Christ's description? (1:13-16)

18. What is John's response to this dazzling vision of Christ? (1:17)

19. What two events in the life of Jesus are referred to by Christ in his first speech to John? (1:18b)

20. As a result of these events, what does Christ possess? (1:18c)

21. What does Christ command John to do? (1:19)

22. What does Christ tell John that the seven golden lamp-stands (1:12-13) and the seven stars (1:16) are symbols for? (1:20)

DIMENSION TWO:
WHAT DOES THE BIBLE MEAN?

❏ *Revelation 1:1-3.* The New Revised Standard Version titles this book "The Revelation to John." The King James Version calls it "The Revelation *of* John." The New International Version simply labels it "Revelation." The opening sentence, however, makes it clear that the revelation given by God is to and of Jesus Christ. The writer of this book, named John, is then given a share of the revelation by Jesus Christ. Is the writer just being humble? Probably not. As you read Revelation carefully, you will discover the central, key position that the exalted Christ plays in the book. Jesus Christ alone is high and lifted up as the One worthy to open the seven seals (5:6-14). Jesus Christ, the One who is "Faithful and True," conquers by the sharp sword of his mouth (19:11-16).

Yet the Christ of John's extraordinary vision is the same as the Jesus of the Gospels. From the beginning John speaks about "the revelation of Jesus Christ" (1:2) and "the testimony of Jesus" (1:9). While this phrase may seem odd, the words and acts of Jesus described in the Gospels could very well be summarized as "the testimony of Jesus." In the Gospel accounts of Matthew, Mark, Luke, and John, we follow eagerly the narrative of Jesus' life. Jesus heals, confronts, teaches, has fellowship with saint and sinner alike, debates, encourages, rebukes, and weeps. He prays, sleeps, and eats. In all that he does and says is to be found "the testimony of Jesus." This testimony is brought to full measure when Jesus endures an unjust and cruel death and is vindicated by God in resurrection from the dead. His whole life and death are "the testimony of Jesus."

What might it mean for us to "take to heart" this testimony as John claims he has done? The answer is explicitly given in the Gospel According to John. There, in his great prayer on behalf of his people, Jesus says to God, "For I gave them the words you gave me and they accepted them. They knew with certainty that I came from you, and they believed that you sent me" (John 17:8).

To take to heart the testimony of Jesus means to dwell on the words of Jesus Christ as conveyed to us through the biblical tradition. However, we cannot merely read these words. Christians must seek to find the meaning of the testimony of Jesus for their lives in every place and in all times. This explains the emphasis, at the very outset of Revelation (1:3), on reading, hearing, and taking to heart the words of Jesus. Likely the function of prophecy in the time of John of Patmos was primarily that of making the words of Jesus fresh and powerful in the present moment. John is doing just that in his visionary report. The revelation belongs to Jesus, not to John. But the prophet is responsible for bringing the revelation to life for the churches.

John describes the revelation given to Jesus Christ as *testimony*. This word will be used many ways throughout the book. To give testimony is the same as to bear witness (1:5a). A witness is one who gives testimony. The Greek word for *martyr* is taken from the same family of words. To die for Jesus is to give testimony to Jesus. Jesus died, was raised, and then became the exalted testimony of God. John is saying here that his testimony is based on Jesus Christ's death and resurrection.

Why does John emphasize the death and resurrection of Jesus (repeated in 1:17-18)? In these two events we see most clearly the divine intention of the Christ event. In the death of Jesus we see the full extent of God's love for humankind. In the Resurrection we see the goal of redemption—the restoration of creation as God intended it to be and the renewal of life for the universe. The powers of evil will, throughout

Revelation, seek to limit and control the salvation won by Jesus Christ in his death and resurrection.

Here, at the very beginning of this drama, the principle is established that in the end the love of God will triumph in the victory of Jesus Christ. As we will see, for John the greatest good a Christian can achieve is to "hold to the testimony of Jesus" (19:10). We get just a hint of what this idea means here. John believes Jesus Christ is alive and continually sharing his message with his servants. To those who listen carefully, Christ still bears witness through his messengers.

❑ *Revelation 1:4-7.* The Book of Revelation starts out very much like other books in the New Testament called epistles or letters. John makes it clear that his message is meant to help local churches. Later he will name these churches (1:11), and each will get a mini-letter. John begins here with a salute ("to the seven churches in the province of Asia"); a greeting ("Grace and peace to you "); and a tribute to the One who is the source of his message, Jesus Christ (1:5). John does not present himself as a "substitute Christ." Rather, John is the one to whom Christ has entrusted a vision of the revelation given to Christ by God.

❑ *Revelation 1:9-11.* John's encounter with "the testimony of Jesus" was a strange and frightening one. John was on an isolated island in the Mediterranean Sea between present-day Greece and Turkey. He was probably banished to Patmos by a cruel Roman emperor. John's life there was harsh, and he was fortunate even to survive. In his banishment John continued to worship God. In the midst of worship, John's terrifying experience of prophecy took place.

This event should give us real pause for reflection. Worship for John was the source of learning. How can liturgy lead to understanding? John suggests here that some mysteries of life can only be understood by means of liturgical worship.

Many people talk about John's strange encounter as a vision. But the experience was more an audition, or hearing, according to John. Perhaps his experience was full of sound because of the pivotal role of "the word of God" in Revelation. Those who enjoy going into a comfortable, quiet room alone to listen to and be carried away by great music will understand how a vision could be mainly auditory. Throughout Revelation sound as much as sight moves John.

❑ *Revelation 1:12-16.* These verses contain a beautiful word picture of the exalted Christ. The images used are meant to give the reader a sense of a dazzling appearance, totally unlike any human or earthly reality. The picture has many common symbols from some of the great visionary experiences of the Old Testament, especially those of Daniel, Isaiah, and Ezekiel. The difference is that all those partial experiences of the divine presence are exceeded by John's encounter with the Christ, the source of all revelation, whose face is "like the sun shining in all its brilliance" (1:16).

❑ *Revelation 1:17-20.* This section portrays a unity, seven being a perfect number. The seven churches are "seven golden lampstands." Why does Christ call the churches *lampstands?* The most important task of the church is to shine like a light set on a lampstand, to bear witness faithfully to "the testimony of Jesus." A lamp on a lampstand is a common biblical symbol for bearing witness (Matthew 5:15).

We may also be surprised to learn that an angel is in every church. Why? Many angels take part in the action of Revelation's drama. They carry out the commands of God by action. The popular view of angels as harp-strumming choristers with little power to engage the real world does not fit here. In the mini-letters of Chapters 2 and 3, Christ addresses the angel, not the congregation.

Some persons have suggested that human agents can be thought of as angels. Maybe the angels in each of the seven churches are really prophets like John. These messengers are expected to carry out the message being given to each congregation. When Christ speaks in heaven, his angels carry out his commands. When John tells of his encounter with "the First and the Last," the angel-prophets of the seven churches are expected to affirm and proclaim the message.

This interpretation certainly can provide us with an interesting viewpoint. The angels of Revelation are powerful, courageous agents of change. They are portrayed consistently in Revelation as being locked in fierce combat with the agents of evil. The angels of the seven churches are told to resist compromise, fear, and all weak-willed desires as a means of remaining faithful to the "testimony of Jesus." So, too, are we.

DIMENSION THREE:
WHAT DOES THE BIBLE MEAN TO ME?

Revelation 1

Can Jesus Christ be a present, living reality today? The most important impression one gets from a prayerful reading of the opening chapter of Revelation is of the profound encounter of John with the risen Christ.

Some people read this encounter with fear, some with envy, some with skepticism. We do wrong to make quick judgments about the spirituality of those who have a practice of faith different from ours. We need to learn this important lesson well. Forgetting it can cause disaster for us and for others. Nothing divides people more firmly than religious prejudice.

The study of Revelation is often a study in religious intolerance and bias. No book in the New Testament has so sharply divided Christians. This division still exists in some places. Such division is truly ironic, since Revelation portrays a dynamic unity of the earth's people.

Can you study this book with an open mind?

Be faithful, even to the point of death, and I will
give you the crown of life (2:10c).

2

Seven Letters to Seven Churches

Revelation 2–3

DIMENSION ONE:
WHAT DOES THE BIBLE SAY?

Answer these questions by reading Revelation 2–3

1. Seven "mini-letters" are sent to seven churches in Asia. Identify the churches. (2:1, 8, 12, 18; 3:1, 7, 14)

2. In each case, to whom is the letter addressed? (2:1, 8, 12, 18; 3:1, 7, 14)

3. Which of these seven churches receives no praise? (3:14-22)

4. Which two churches receive only praise and no censure? (2:8-11; 3:7-13)

5. What are some reasons for churches being praised? (2:2, 9, 13, 19; 3:8)

6. Each church receives a promise on the basis of doing what? (2:7, 11, 17, 26; 3:5, 12, 21)

7. What are some of the good things promised to those who conquer? (2:7, 11, 17, 26-28; 3:5, 12, 21)

8. Who provides the model of what it means to conquer? (3:21)

9. What exhortation closes all the mini-letters? (2:7, 11, 17, 29; 3:6, 13, 22)

10. Who are some of the people censured? (2:2, 6, 9, 14-15, 20; 3:9, 17)

11. What are some of the provocative images John uses to describe things Christ censures? (2:4; 3:2-4, 15, 17)

12. The church at Laodicea is asked to do several things to be acceptable to Christ. What are these things? (3:18-19)

13. How is Christ described in the opening words of the seven letters? (2:1, 8, 12, 18; 3:1, 7, 14)

DIMENSION TWO: WHAT DOES THE BIBLE MEAN?

The two chapters of Revelation containing the seven mini-letters to the churches (2–3) are a family document. When we write close friends and relatives, we often write in a kind of shorthand. This shorthand is a way of writing that we use when the other person knows a great deal about us and our loved ones. We can imagine someone writing that "Uncle Bob is having his same old trouble again. We sure do wish he could get on his feet, once and for all." Anyone outside the family reading such a line would have no way of knowing what Uncle Bob's chronic problem is, nor could that person figure out just what it would mean for him to "get on his feet" permanently.

The same thing is true of this part of Revelation. Even the most knowledgeable scholars do not know for sure who the Jezebel in the letter to Thyatira might have been (2:20); and we cannot be certain what it means, spiritually, to soil one's clothes (3:4). Clearly, however, in these letters the risen Christ is calling his churches to faithful obedience.

As you answered the questions in Dimension One, you saw the rich variety of images used to describe the blessings Christ wants to give his people. To receive these gifts, we must conquer. But what do we conquer, and how? The answer is different in each case. These seven mini-letters make it clear that each situation is different. This fact should encourage us who want to benefit from Revelation.

Christians are expected to see the dangers, temptations, and blind spots of their situation for what they are. Christians are also expected to overcome their situation. They are expected to be victorious in their circumstance, whatever it might be. When Christians are victorious, they receive blessings so great they can hardly be described.

❏ *Revelation 2:1-7. The Church in Ephesus.* This church gets a mixed message. Christ praises the Ephesians for resisting evil and for carrying on in difficult circumstances with patience. This church is especially recognized for being able to "keep on keeping on." But they have lost their first love. Perhaps the Ephesians have lost the spontaneous character of their faith. Perhaps prayer, witnessing, liturgy, and fellowship with other Christians have become a matter of habit.

Why would one abandon a first love? In the first days of being in Christ, many believers cannot get enough of that which draws them closer to Christ: prayer, Bible study, devoted service to the community and church. This early "love affair" was probably expressed in many ways by the Ephesians. Without doubt their first love meant seeking to understand better the fullness of Christ. But the Ephesians might have become lackluster in their faithfulness. They need to go back to the freshness of their first love.

❏ *Revelation 2:8-11. The Church in Smyrna.* This church receives nothing but praise. Yet they are in danger—from outside the church. Quite probably they are under continual threat from civil authorities. They are risking jail daily. They are poor as well. These Christians are portrayed as without adequate food, shelter, and protection from oppressive forces. Many will die. Yet they are encouraged to remain faithful, even in death. Verse 11 has a subtle reminder that even if the enemies of Christ succeed in killing the Christians at Smyrna once, the Christians will not die again but share in Christ's resurrection (2:8). Jesus died but came to life. These Christians may also die. If they do, they will live again. In a parallel fashion they may be economically poor, but they are rich. They have an inheritance. They will receive a royal crown; and with Christ, they will reign in life.

SEVEN LETTERS TO SEVEN CHURCHES **13**

❑ *Revelation 2:12-17. The Church in Pergamum.* This church is both praised and rebuked. They have shown their spiritual insight and moral courage in the past by remaining loyal to Christ in hard times. A local Christian hero (Antipas) is recalled by name. Mentioning Antipas probably reminds the people receiving this letter of an entire history of pain, suffering, and death. Antipas is not mentioned elsewhere, but we can safely assume that he was a trusted Christian leader who stood up against evil and was killed for his witness.

The largest part of the message, however, is directed against Christians who are teaching the doctrines of "the Nicolaitans" (2:15). While we do not know much about this group, probably they taught a doctrine of compromise. This teaching may have included a working out of rationalizations for Christians taking part in pagan practices and rituals without feeling guilty. Their teaching may have concerned a matter as seemingly simple as shopping in the Roman marketplace for meat that had previously been ritually offered to pagan gods (2:14).

The reference to Balaam probably has as its major point of comparison the idea of scandal or temptation to sin. Perhaps the sin of idolatry that Balaam taught Balak, the Moabite king, is the point of comparison. (See Numbers 22–24 for the complete story.)

Where does Revelation stand on the question of compromise? Throughout the book all weakening of faith by even the smallest compromise is condemned. This attitude has real wisdom. Persons who have personally experienced oppression will understand that small compromises made under the fear of loss inevitably lead to larger compromises until no retreat is left and one has sold one's soul to evil. Revelation's viewpoint may seem hard-line and unreasonably inflexible, but subsequent Christian experience has demonstrated its wisdom.

❑ *Revelation 2:18-29. The Church in Thyatira.* Thyatira is censured for putting up with "Jezebel." The original Jezebel was the queen consort of King Ahab in the Old Testament. The stories told of her give a grudging respect for her loyal efforts on behalf of her god, Baal. (Her constant battle with Elijah, recorded in First Kings [16:31; 18:3–19:1; 21], has given us some of the liveliest stories in Scripture.) We know nothing for certain about the Christian prophetess John calls Jezebel. But John's frequent use of Old Testament stories, names, and images makes us wonder why he calls this woman Jezebel. Whoever she was, perhaps she was a powerful and clever opponent of John. Other passages in Revelation show us that John cuts a fine line when it comes to matters of belief. Her witness to faith is challenged by John. He portrays here the beginnings of a major church argument.

❏ *Revelation 3:1-6. The Church in Sardis.* This church receives little good news. They think they are alive, but they are dead! They are in danger of really dying. This church has completely misunderstood the life to which Christ has called his people. They have accepted a standard of discipleship quite unacceptable to Christ. The image of soiled clothes suggests that moral issues are at stake. They have given in too easily to the rich temptations posed by their environment.

❏ *Revelation 3:7-13. The Church in Philadelphia.* This church has learned to be great in its weakness. This principle is close to the heart of the gospel. Frequently, Jesus proclaimed that the small, weak, and unsophisticated of this world will confound the great, strong, and wise. How interesting that this little church captures the essential core of Christ's teaching and holds on against all odds.

❏ *Revelation 3:14-22. The Church in Laodicea.* Perhaps the clearest picture of the seven churches is this one. Quite unlike the Smyrna Christians, these Christians have prospered along with the Roman city of Laodicea. This prosperity has created a dangerous condition of spiritual apathy.

John creates here a firm bridge between the Gospels and Revelation. He sees great risk in economic wealth. But the reason for wealth being a danger is described differently by the risen Christ in Revelation than it is by Jesus of Nazareth in Matthew, Mark, and Luke. Here Christ is portrayed by John as saying, in effect, "Your economic wealth has blinded you to my wealth. I possess gold of the purest kind; rich garments; and precious, rare medicines. You must find a way to buy these from me." Christ is, in effect, a divine merchant with expensive goods to sell.

The terms of the sale are consistent with the message of Jesus in the Gospels. In fact, John uses almost identical words to those spoken by Jesus in Matthew 7:7-8 and Luke 11:9-10. To get the gold, the garments, and the miraculous cure for blindness, one need only ask.

Here we see the inner workings of economic wealth. The problem with riches is not a moral one. In the biblical view wealth is a danger only because it seems always to lead its captives to believe that they are clothed when they are naked, have sight when they are blind, are blessed when they are cursed, and are enviable when they are pitiable. Wealth is a great deceiver. Much of Revelation seeks to make it clear that the obvious is not always the most real. To live victoriously, Christians must look beneath the surface.

DIMENSION THREE:
WHAT DOES THE BIBLE MEAN TO ME?

Right Belief and Right Action

Does it really matter what you believe? Does it matter how you live?

Most people are less concerned about holding the right religious doctrines and more concerned about how they and others act. "What you do speaks more loudly than what you say" is a common way of gently confronting others when people get too smug about how right they think they are. Christians are often accused of hypocrisy. Literally, *hypocrisy* means wearing a mask. The Book of Revelation strips away the masks of hypocrisy.

These mini-letters must have had a chilling effect on those who heard them for the first time. John says that life itself is at stake in what people do. How can we know when we are being hypocritical? How does Christ speak to you and to your church?

Christians have often been known for the things they argue about among themselves. Sometimes this infighting has greatly diminished the witness of Christianity in the eyes of those outside the church. Often these church arguments have been over unworthy, petty issues and doctrinal hairsplitting. At other times these disputes have concerned matters of urgency for the entire world.

We may assume that the issues John raised in these mini-letters were of great importance. Quite likely the survival of the Christian witness in Asia Minor was at stake. How can we, today, separate the petty, nonessential disputes between Christian groups from those of global significance? Can you identify some of each? Is it wrong for Christians to disagree with one another over important issues? How do we maintain fellowship and dialogue when we do honestly disagree?

Worthy is the Lamb, who was slain,
to receive power and wealth and wisdom and strength
and honor and glory and praise! (5:12).

—— 3 ——
Worthy Is the Lamb
Revelation 4–5

DIMENSION ONE:
WHAT DOES THE BIBLE SAY?

Answer these questions by reading Revelation 4

1. What did John see and hear? (4:1)

2. How did John get to heaven? (4:2)

3. How many thrones did John see? (4:2-4)

4. How were the elders dressed? (4:4b)

5. Who else is present at this throne scene? (4:5-7)

6. What is the function of the twenty-four elders and the four living creatures? (4:8-11)

7. What has God done to be worthy of such praise? (4:11)

Answer these questions by reading Revelation 5

8. What did John see? (5:1-2, 6)

9. Who is the mighty angel looking for? (5:2)

10. Can anyone open the seals? (5:3)

11. Who finally is found to open the seals? (5:5)

12. What does the Lamb do? (5:7)

13. What happens when the Lamb takes the scroll? (5:8-9)

14. In the new song, what is it that makes the Lamb worthy to open the seals? (5:9-10)

15. How many angels respond in praise of the Lamb? (5:11)

16. Do only the elders and angels sing praise? (5:13-14)

DIMENSION TWO:
WHAT DOES THE BIBLE MEAN?

From this point on John experiences the extraordinary sights and sounds of Revelation. His description of what he sees and hears is what makes this book so unusual in the New Testament. As you read and study this unique book, keep in mind what it is, the report of an unusual spiritual experience. John is transported "in the Spirit" (1:10 and 4:2) that he might hear and see realities hidden to others.

The images John uses to explain his encounters often reveal that mere words are inadequate to capture his impressions fully. Sometimes, for example, his comparisons are difficult to pin down. Yet John is a prophet who is obviously right at home in the Hebrew Scriptures. Almost every image, every phrase, and every literary device he uses comes from another biblical writer. In these two chapters alone he uses word pictures, descriptions, and ideas from several Old Testament books: Genesis, Exodus, Psalms, Isaiah, Daniel, Zechariah, and especially Ezekiel. In fact, if you were to sit down for an hour or two and read the Old Testament Book of Ezekiel, you would be surprised how much of it John uses to capture his spiritual experience.

❏ *Revelation 4:1-8a.* These verses could be described as the "Throne Room Scene." John's experience began with hearing a voice "like a trumpet" (1:10). His description probably is an attempt to capture the sense of a clear, sharp, insistent quality of voice. This voice now shows John an open door. The open door means that he is being invited to enter. In fact, John is openly invited to visit heaven. This invitation, though remarkable, is actually typical of the ecstatic experiences of prophets like John. He is going to visit the Source of all revelation, the place where God dwells. The fact that John is permitted to visit God in heaven is meant subtly to suggest that his vision is to be taken seriously. Who can doubt his vision if it has come from God's presence?

The description of the throne room is exciting. John does not even try to describe the appearance of God. John only talks about color and light. God is not to be imagined in form, for this would be idolatry. Like a good Old Testament prophet (such as Ezekiel in his first vision [1:26-28a]), John pictures God as a combination of brilliant colors. The *jasper* is composed of earth tones, the *carnelian* is a deep red, and the *emerald* is a brilliant green. God is completely "other," not resembling human creation, and is best described visually as a flashing spectrum of color. So the best interpreters of this passage have been artists of various kinds.

The twenty-four elders are the redeemed of Christ who live in heaven with God. We have already seen that the white robe and golden crown are the inheritance of the righteous (2:10; 3:4, 18).

The four living creatures are described almost exactly as Ezekiel described them (Ezekiel 1:5-14) but with more economy and less terror. As a unity, they represent the wholeness of God's creation. They are meant to symbolize nature in its fullness. Because nature reflects the glory of God, descriptions of the four living creatures tell us something about God. For example, the abundance of eyes (4:8) speaks of God's complete knowledge of all things. Portraying humankind as a partner with other animals—lion, ox, and eagle—may be a way of saying, "We're all in this together." Not only human beings, but all the created order seek the face of God.

❑ *Revelation 4:8b-11.* The Christians who have been redeemed and the representatives of the created order are in heaven for one reason. They give glory to God in continual worship. This focus on liturgy and worship is important to an understanding of Revelation.

Artists have made the best use of Revelation through the centuries. At times this book has been scoffed at, neglected, and even rejected by theologians. But poets, visual artists, and musicians have seen an inner beauty in Revelation. We can see why. This book gives equal value to sight and sound. One cannot understand Revelation without a lively, artistic imagination. John's rich and variegated images and word pictures draw us into Revelation's orbit. The place of art and music in liturgy explains the link between Revelation and those who live by art. Taken at face value, Revelation reveals the proper focus of existence, the praise of God. All life is to be interpreted as the expressive adoration of God. Here is the proper realm of the artist and musician.

John presents two topics in the worship of God: (1) God exists forever (4:8), and (2) God is the cause of all that exists (4:11). The two ideas are closely linked. If you think about it for a moment, you will realize that time itself is a creation. Therefore, if God is the Creator, God must exist beyond time. God is greater than time. God creates time. Our certainty that all things are under God's care must include time. Before time existed, God existed. God will also care for all that is when time ceases to be.

John wants to establish this certainty here. Soon the events of Revelation will begin to march toward the final curtain. Life will change at some point; and when it does, God will still be "the Lord God Almighty" (4:8). But John takes one more step. Worship is the only appropriate activity for all creation—including humankind—simply because all existence is a gift of God. God is and has caused to be all that is and all that will be. Our best response to this dominant fact of existence is to worship and glorify the Creator. Worship is the most authentic response of life.

These two chapters paint a mood of expectancy. The sense of a calm before the storm grows with every sentence of Chapter 5.

❑ *Revelation 5:1-8.* John now introduces the scroll with seven seals. As we will see, what is written on the scroll is never revealed. In fact, the scroll itself is not of great importance. The seven seals on the edge of the rolled scroll are important.

John hints at a kind of Olympic contest of both heaven and earth's best. We can imagine that many try to break the seal, but none can. The quality being searched for is "worthy" (5:4). We will learn later how *worthy* is defined.

John is so much a part of the drama that he sees himself weeping. He is caught up in such a way that the reader forgets John is supposed to be an observer.

If you did not know the Bible very well, you would probably not recognize "the Lion of the tribe of Judah, the Root of David" as Jesus Christ. He will open the seals; and as this happens, the action of Revelation unfolds.

Jesus appears as the Lamb of God. The Lamb is a favorite image for Jesus in Revelation. You may think lambs are gentle and sweet. The idea in Revelation, however, is connected with lambs as Passover sacrifices. This image implies blood and pain. Both in Revelation and in the Gospel of John, Jesus dies as the Passover lamb. (This sacrifice takes place before Passover actually begins, on the eve of preparation.) By dying as the Passover lamb before Passover, Jesus brings to perfect completion the salvation promised Israel in the Passover. The original Passover in Egypt provided a means of protection for the Hebrews on the night of God's judgment on Egypt. Those with the blood of the lamb on the doorpost were saved from the destruction of the first-born (Exodus 12). The death of Jesus on the cross signals the salvation of all humankind.

Jesus is the "Lamb, [who was] slain"; and only Jesus is permitted to approach God. When others tried to open the scroll, a "mighty angel" intervened. But Jesus has complete access to God's right hand.

The elders and creatures we met in Chapter 4 respond to Jesus, the Lamb, in exactly the same way they did to God. They fall down in worship. Jesus is God.

❏ *Revelation 5:9-14.* The hymn of praise of Jesus also starts out with the words "You are worthy" (5:9). Why is Jesus worthy? For much the same reason God is worthy. By his redeeming death as the Passover lamb, Jesus has created a new people. This new people is drawn from all humanity. They are, together, a kingdom of the righteous. They are righteous, not because of what they have done, but because they have been redeemed. Jesus has perfectly completed God's salvation: He is worthy.

But now new voices join in the song. A countless number ("thousands upon thousands, and ten thousand times ten thousand") of angels sing with a "loud voice." Now heaven and earth are joined together in praise of the Lamb. John has a reason for his portrayal of cosmic unity. Only with the fullness of Christ's work can God's created order be fulfilled. In Christ all things are made complete.

The Lamb's work extends beyond his earthly sojourn as Jesus of Nazareth. Here, something new is revealed to John: Jesus, the Christ, continues in heavenly existence to bring about the completeness of redemption. This astounding insight may be overshadowed by the interest we take in the violent action of the story that follows.

The continual struggle of Jesus on behalf of the people of God is a rich idea. Jesus' struggle not only has the power to sustain those who suffer greatly for their faith, it also deepens our understanding of salvation. It is not simply an accomplished fact but a dynamic reality.

DIMENSION THREE:
WHAT DOES THE BIBLE MEAN TO ME?

Revelation 4:1-8

At one time our popular culture would have scoffed at this word picture of John's unusual spiritual experience. But in an era when fantasy of all kinds in music, films, and literature has captivated the imaginations of many, the imagery in Revelation may seem mild by comparison. Some people think of the Bible as a dry, even boring, book. No one could read this passage with care and still be bored. But this story is no mere fantasy. John reports, not imagines, his experiences at the throne of God; and his insights are confirmed by the whole of Scripture.

Revelation 4:9-11

One of the key convictions of John's account of what happens in heaven is that all creatures exist for the single purpose of giving praise to God. We live and breathe and have our being to glorify the God who created us. This perspective on life can be liberating, if we allow it to be. Under this attitude we can freely live each day as our way of thanking God for the gift of life. At the end of each day, we can offer our efforts up to God as our gift of thanksgiving. How long has it been since you tried to live consciously in the praise of God in all that you do and say?

Revelation 5:1-5

Jesus appears here as the great champion of heaven. He was victorious in his life and death. His victory has won a new people. We are that people, and great things are expected of us. But these expectations are based on the conquest of Jesus Christ. Because he has conquered, we no longer need fear the outcome of history. To what challenge is God calling you? How can we view our present life as a contest in which we must, like Christ, be champions?

Revelation 5:6-14

If God and the Lamb are worthy, then our future is secured. How can this follow? Can it really be true that we need not fear the future if they are worthy? John is suggesting a simple but profound logic here. If the Lord God Almighty exists before, during, and after time and if this Lord really has been the cause of all that has come to be, then all things are under the care of God. This being so, the only thing that remains is this question: Do you choose to sing, "To him who sits on the throne and to the Lamb / be praise and honor and glory and power, for ever and ever!"? If we as a priestly people have been ransomed by Jesus' blood and if we have been made into a kingdom devoted to the service of God by Christ, then our welfare rests in the victory of the Lamb.

—— 4 ——
The Book of
the Seven Seals
Revelation 6–7

DIMENSION ONE:
WHAT DOES THE BIBLE SAY?

Answer these questions by reading Revelation 6

1. What happens when the Lamb opens the first seal? (6:1-2)

2. What does the rider of the white horse do? (6:2)

3. What happens when the Lamb opens the second seal? (6:3-4a)

4. What happens to the rider of the red horse? (6:4bc)

5. What happens when the Lamb opens the third seal? (6:5)

6. What does the rider of the black horse do? (6:6)

7. What happens when the Lamb opens the fourth seal? (6:7-8a)

8. What does the rider of the pale horse do? (6:8bc)

9. What did John see when the fifth seal was opened? (6:9-11)

10. What happened when the sixth seal was opened? (6:12-17)

Answer these questions by reading Revelation 7

11. What happens at the opening of Chapter 7? (7:1)

12. What takes place in the next scene? (7:2-3)

13. How many of God's servants are sealed, and how is the number determined? (7:4-8)

14. Where does the next scene take place? (7:9)

15. Who is present that we have not seen before? (7:9)

16. How did this group get to heaven? (7:13-14)

17. What is given to this great multitude? (7:15-17)

DIMENSION TWO:
WHAT DOES THE BIBLE MEAN?

Revelation 6 and 7 describe the events that the breaking of the first six seals of the scroll set in motion. These events take place in heaven and on earth, continuing the theme of the interaction between heaven and earth. The images of these chapters have been the inspiration of poets, musicians, artists, and religious leaders for centuries. The importance of these ideas in the history of Christianity is hard to exaggerate.

❑ *Revelation 6:1-8.* While a sequence of events is suggested by this narrative of John's vision, we must be constantly aware of the simultaneous nature of John's vision. A rush of action greets us in the breaking of the first four seals. We are almost encouraged to imagine the seals being popped open with a sliding motion of the hand as it moves down the scroll. One destruction follows quickly upon the other.

Each of the four horsemen is called forth by the command of a living creature: *"Come!"* The action following each command is swift and sketched with a minimum of words. We are left to supply with our imaginations the terrible details of destruction and suffering that follow in the wake of each awesome horse and rider. While the commands come from heaven, the consequences fall on earth. For the first time in the Book of Revelation, earth receives the impact of actions initiated in heaven.

❑ *Revelation 6:9-11.* The explicit prayer for vengeance is at first shocking. As sovereign Lord, God is committed to judge all humans (including Christians). The petition of the martyred saints is that God will speed judgment, and the result of this will be to "avenge our blood." John's words here are consistent with the apocalyptic viewpoint of both Paul (Romans 12:19) and Jesus (Luke 21:22). John is describing a final judgment in which the righteous will be vindicated and the unjust punished.

❑ *Revelation 6:12-17.* We often hear people speak of "acts of God." This phrase usually means violent weather, earthquakes, floods, and other phenomena of nature. Here nature turns against humankind. In the Bible eclipses of the sun, earthquakes, and floods are all seen as acts caused by God. Often these events are not seen as important in themselves. Rather, they demonstrate God's control over nature and history. Or these events can be seen as signs that reveal God. For example, some of the events spoken of here are similar to those reported to have taken place at the death of Jesus on the cross (Matthew 27:45-54).

The events told of here, however, are more devastating than a local earthquake or two. These are not simply signs. In the description of the opening of the sixth seal, existence itself is threatened. Islands of the sea break loose, and entire mountain ranges are leveled. The heavens are changed beyond recognition. All humanity recognizes this as the judgment of God and the beginning of another, less reliable, kind of life.

❑ *Revelation 7:1-8.* This passage is presented as an interlude in the action of death and destruction resulting from the breaking of seals. John's poetic description of the four winds of earth is a metaphor for *calm*. The wind is calm, and we are to feel calm as we look over the shoulder of John and see what he sees.

The idea of sealing or stamping the forehead is an ancient one, still used in some cultures. We are not told what the mark looked like. Clearly, however, the mark identifies these tribes as "servants of our God."

The Book of Revelation is fond of symbolic numbers. Here 144,000 is the result of a mathematical "piling up" of perfection. Twelve is fullness; even more full would be 12 times 12; and 12 multiplied by 12,000 is 144,000. The point is that the people of God are preserved from total destruction. This fact gives reassurance to those reading this prophecy who may have been asking, "Who then can survive?" The forehead mark, however, does not protect the people of God from death; it is a sign of their identity as a part of God's people.

❑ *Revelation 7:9-14.* The size of the company ("a great multitude that no one could count" [7:9]) suggests that yet some time is to elapse before the hard times of the redeemed will be complete. In 6:11, the reader is told that "the number" of those who will yet be numbered must be " completed." Here, John is allowed to see ahead, when the number will be complete. The number he sees is similar to the number of angels praising God (5:11): Their number is countless, in the "ten thousand times ten thousand."

Revelation describes a global and universal throng. They are "from every nation, tribe, people and language" (7:9). Salvation is for all peoples and cultures.

Revelation has often been forced to serve the interests of a single group. Actually, the perspective of Revelation is more universal and inclusive than many other parts of Scripture. Although the prophecy of Revelation begins with a focus on seven Asian churches, we are quickly led to realize that the church throughout the world—even including as yet unknown churches—is what concerns John.

By now we are well acquainted with the white robe of redemption. The interesting way John uses the idea of color is illustrated in 7:14, where the red blood of the Lamb makes robes white. The point of color in Revelation is often not tint but the effect color creates.

The acclamation given God and the Lamb (7:10) by the hosts of the redeemed is especially important in this passage. "Salvation belongs to our God." The point of this praise of God is that God is the source of salvation. Those who praise God for salvation are those who have suffered and died in tribulation (7:14). Salvation therefore includes their final victory over death. This victory is symbolized by their white robes and their participation in the liturgy around the heavenly throne.

❑ *Revelation 7:15-17.* This beautiful poetic passage is really a preview of a more lengthy and detailed description of the new heaven and new earth in Revelation 21. Again we meet an idea essential to the theology of Revelation: The fulfillment of life's promise for humankind (and all creation) is the service of God. This service is identical with liturgy, the praise and honoring of God in music and song.

The images John uses to describe the life of those wearing the white robes are deeply moving. Satisfaction of hunger, thirst, and grief would not seem to be relevant to heavenly existence. John uses the known to explain the unknown, however. Perhaps no hunger, thirst, grief, or sunstroke will exist in heaven; but all these things speak of the harshness of life. The redeemed with Christ will be free of these painful and unwelcome dimensions of existence that at times seek to destroy the joy of living. The meanings of these images of liberation are limitless in their possibilities. For example, the scorching heat of the sun could well be a metaphor for the debilitating experience of a chronic illness, the terrible effects of grinding physical work, or the terror of emotional stress and illness.

DIMENSION THREE:
WHAT DOES THE BIBLE MEAN TO ME?

Revelation 6:1-8

Everything described in the breaking of the first four seals has been experienced in every century since the writing of Revelation. Although most of us live in a protected environment, the turmoil and suffering caused by famine, epidemics, wars, and natural catastrophes is made real by seeing them on television. John saw the hand of God in these disasters. Do you think we ought to interpret these disasters as carrying out the will of God? Why, or why not?

Revelation 6:9-11

At one time it was popular to ask gathered Christians to affirm whether they were "willing to die for Christ." We now recognize that an affirmative reply to this question can be dangerous. We have learned that certain kinds of Christian service are almost certain to end with death. While most people reading this book live in a society that guarantees freedom of religious expression, martyrdom has not disappeared. Martyrdom survives under a different guise. Those who choose to work in violent neighborhoods, missionaries to violence-prone countries, and health care specialists dealing with communicable diseases are but a few examples of those who knowingly choose to confess Christ at the real risk of an early death. How does your Christian commitment compare with people such as these? Do you believe that all Christians are called to sacrifice themselves in order to save others? What other risks may be involved in a Christian commitment?

Revelation 6:12-16

A constant theme in Revelation is that God's role will eventually result in a great leveling out of artificial differences. Under God's reign as righteous Judge no difference among persons will exist. Why do we live in a way that suggests this is not the case?

Revelation 7

We are promised relief from all life's harsh disappointments. But this reward cannot be earned. The reward is the outcome of God's wisdom at work in history. The source of salvation is God alone (7:10). Do you believe that the promise is a realistic hope? Is it sufficient as a means of dealing with the real suffering of life? What problems do you see in affirming this kind of faith?

The seven angels who had the seven trumpets
prepared to sound them (8:6).

5

The Seven Trumpets

Revelation 8–9

DIMENSION ONE:
WHAT DOES THE BIBLE SAY?

Answer these questions by reading Revelation 8

1. What takes place when the seventh seal is opened? (8:1)

2. What happens immediately after the silence? (8:2)

3. What two objects does the other angel have? (8:3)

4. What rises and mingles with the smoke of the censer? (8:4)

5. What happens when the angel takes fire from the altar and throws it on the earth? (8:5)

6. What is the next series of seven to be introduced? (8:6)

7. What happens following the blowing of the first trumpet? (8:7)

8. What happens when the second trumpet is blown? (8:8-9)

9. What happens when the third trumpet is sounded? (8:10-11)

10. What happens when the angel blows the fourth trumpet? (8:12)

11. Does the action of trumpet blowing continue? (8:13)

Answer these questions by reading Revelation 9

12. The sounding of the fifth trumpet sets in motion what event? (9:1-3)

13. How are these creatures limited in their torture? (9:4-5a)

14. How is their terrible work described? (9:5b-6)

15. How would you describe these creatures? (9:7-10)

16. Who is their king? (9:11)

17. How else are the last three trumpets described? (9:12)

18. What other group of numbers is introduced when the sixth trumpet is blown? (9:13-14)

19. What do these destroying angels do? (9:15)

20. What are the troops of these angels like? (9:16-19)

21. What is the effect of these woes or plagues on those who are not killed? (9:20-21)

DIMENSION TWO:
WHAT DOES THE BIBLE MEAN?

By now you are getting used to having events happen in a series of seven. When the seventh seal is opened, we find another seven, seven trumpets. Revelation 8 and 9 narrate the action following the blowing of six of the trumpets. You also are getting used to having these series of seven interrupted. An interruption takes place here after the blowing of the sixth trumpet (9:13). Two additional scenes follow. These scenes present the bittersweet scroll of Revelation 10 and the two prophets of Revelation 11. Not until the end of the vision concerning the two prophets is the seventh trumpet blown (11:15).

❏ *Revelation 8:1-5.* Silence is not simply the absence of sound. Silence can be a powerful and meaningful reality, which is the case here. We might have expected yet another scene in which the hosts of heaven offer God and the Lamb unceasing praise. Instead there is silence. Why? Most of this passage concerns the golden altar and the burning of incense that mingles with the prayers of the saints. A Jewish tradition suggests that silence in heaven is kept so that the prayers of God's people on earth can be better heard.

The idea of incense being "visual prayer" is a beautiful one. Remember that in an earlier scene we saw, with John, the prayers of the saints portrayed in the same way, as "golden bowls full of incense" (5:8). We should also remember that the martyred souls dwelling at the foot of the altar cry for the vengeance of God's judgment (6:9-10). The prayer rising as incense in a profound silence is a cry for justice. Both those believers who have been murdered and those who are still alive—but suffer under terrible persecution—petition God for a swift end to this torment. The events that follow are partial answers to the pleas of the martyrs and saints.

❏ *Revelation 8:6-13. The First Four Trumpets.* The first four trumpets are similar to one another. They describe the partial destruction of the world of nature. First the vegetation is partially destroyed, then the oceans of salt, then fresh water, then the celestial lights. In each case humankind suffers as a result of nature's destruction. The idea of "a third" is probably not meant to be a precise fraction. Rather, this figure suggests that life for humans and for nature does not end but becomes nearly unbearable.

Parts of these visions are more realistic to us than they were to the original readers. We have seen what happens when huge oil spills devastate areas of the ocean and its coastlands. We are also familiar with the projections of a "nuclear winter" or of "global warming" in which the sun's light might either be partially blocked or let through the atmosphere without filtering, creating conditions in nature that destroy life.

❏ *Revelation 9:1-11. The Fifth Trumpet.* The action following the blowing of this trumpet begins with a story based on ancient traditions about fallen angels. Often these angels are pictured as stars in heaven. When an angel sins, a star "falls." In order to control such evil angels, God locks them in bottomless pits, where they can do no harm. This is the picture here. We are even told the name of this fallen angel: He is "Abaddon" (9:11). The name has no history to it. In all ancient literature the name only shows up here. Abaddon in Hebrew means simply "destruction" or "The Destroyer." The Greek name ("Apollyon") is merely a translation of the Hebrew word.

When the bottomless pit is opened, a boiling pack of fantastic creatures is let loose on human beings. We are meant to use our imaginations when it comes to the description of these "locusts." The main point of these locusts is that they inflict enough pain to make victims wish they were dead (9:5-6).

❏ *Revelation 9:13-19. The Sixth Trumpet.* This vision also involves demonic, otherworldly creatures of torment. They wound like a dreaded animal, the poisonous snake (9:19b). The difference is, they also can kill (9:18).

These creatures come from the land of the East, near the river Euphrates. This land is the area of present-day Iraq and Iran; and it was from these lands that the most dreaded enemies of Rome came, the Parthians. Almost every nation has its most feared enemy, and in the mind of many these enemies are superhuman in their power to inflict cruelty.

This huge army of cavalry carries with it that idea. They are described as cavalry (9:16) simply to convey the idea that they came swiftly, relentlessly, and with a terrifying noise like that of tens of thousands of hooves charging at the gallop.

❏ *Revelation 9:20-21.* Perhaps you are not surprised that all this pain and destruction does not cause those who are left alive to repent. If so, it is probably because you are familiar with the history of the Old Testament prophets. Again and again, prophets like Jeremiah predicted devastation on the people of Israel for their sins against the covenant made at Sinai. Not only did the people not listen, they did not repent when the terrible things they were warned about did happen. The same was true of Jesus and John the Baptist. They came to preach repentance and forgiveness of sins (Matthew 3:1-10; 4:17), but the majority did not listen.

John's vision confirms this history and heightens it. He is saying that even if one third of the land, water, heavens, and humankind were to be destroyed by the hand of God, those remaining would probably not repent.

We are reminded of Luke's parable of the poor man, Lazarus (16:19-31). When the rich man in Hades asked Abraham to send Lazarus to warn his living brothers of the dangers that awaited them in death, he was told, "They have Moses and the Prophets; let them listen to them." When the rich man objected that these witnesses were not credible enough, he was told, "If they do not listen to Moses and the Prophets, they will not be convinced even if someone rises from the dead."

The Bible often reflects on the problem of why people do not listen to prophets. The lack of repentance on the part of those remaining alive after the sounding of the first six trumpets will be dealt with in Revelation 10 and 11. The answer is a study on the history of the prophets.

DIMENSION THREE:
WHAT DOES THE BIBLE MEAN TO ME?

How does it make you feel when you read about all the pain, suffering, and death in Revelation? Does it seem strange to you that all this comes as a result of God's judgment? Does it bother you that Revelation sees God in the eventual destruction of animals, plant life, and human beings? In almost every part of the Bible, God is seen, at times, as a God of judgment. In Revelation, God's judgment is found on virtually every page.

Many people understand Revelation as speaking only about the future. Does it seem to you that some of the things described in Revelation 8 and 9 have taken place over and over? Look again at the first four trumpet disasters. What has happened in your lifetime that relates to some of these?

Try the same thing with the description of the next two trumpet disasters. Forget the animal imagery for a moment and ask yourself, *What instruments of war have already been used to produce the kind of suffering described in Revelation 9?*

Chapter 9 also deals with the vivid image of a deep pit with a locked lid over it. In this pit is a boiling chaos of evil. When the lid is lifted by the fallen angel, we could say literally that "all hell breaks loose." The pit is exactly that: a living hell. In your lifetime have you seen some "lids over hell" lifted that have resulted in pain, injustice, and unbearable human conflict? If so, what are they?

You must prophesy again about many peoples, nations,
languages and kings (10:11).

—— **6** ——

A Scroll Both
Bitter and Sweet
Revelation 10–11

DIMENSION ONE:
WHAT DOES THE BIBLE SAY?

Answer these questions by reading Revelation 10

1. How is the "mighty angel" of John's vision described? (10:1)

2. What is the angel holding? (10:2a)

3. Where is the angel standing? (10:2b)

4. After John hears the seven thunders, he is told by another voice not to do what? (10:4)

5. What has the "mighty angel" come to do in John's presence? (10:5-6)

6. What will happen, according to this angel, when the seventh trumpet is sounded? (10:7)

7. What is John instructed to do with the scroll? (10:9)

8. What happens when John eats the scroll? (10:10)

9. What is John told this action means? (10:11)

Answer these questions by reading Revelation 11

10. What is John told to do in this vision? (11:1)

11. How long will "the Gentiles" be permitted to "trample on the holy city" (Jerusalem)? (11:2)

12. Who is given "power . . . to prophesy" for 1,260 days in sackcloth? (11:3)

13. How else are these two witnesses described? (11:4, 10)

14. What kinds of things are the witnesses given power to do? (11:5-6)

15. What happens when their testimony is finished? (11:7-8)

16. What happens to their bodies? (11:9-10)

17. What happens later to the bodies of the two prophets? (11:11-12)

18. What follows this remarkable event? (11:13)

19. Are the people of earth affected by the blowing of the seventh trumpet? (11:15-19)

20. What do the elders thank God for in their hymn of praise? (11:17-18)

21. What new object in the heavenly precincts is introduced? (11:19)

DIMENSION TWO:
WHAT DOES THE BIBLE MEAN?

❏ *Revelation 10:1-2.* The prophet John introduces yet another angel. Clearly this is a colossal angel of truly gigantic proportions. When John says that the angel has "his right foot on the sea and his left foot on the land" (10:2b), we are meant to picture the angel as enormous.

The visual impression creates the kind of image we are becoming familiar with in Revelation. The points of comparison are not meant to be taken literally but are rather intended to help us form a mental picture. For example, this colossal angel has a face "like the sun" and legs "like fiery pillars" (10:1). From this we can create a picture of an angel whose face shines so brightly it cannot be looked at directly and whose legs are rippling as with flames of fiery red. John's description does not mean that the angel's legs were on fire. Rather, the flickering, pulsating character of fire is what is meant. The angel comes shrouded in the mists of a cloud and with a kind of halo around his head, bearing the colors of the rainbow.

We expect angels to bring messages, and this colossal angel does not disappoint us. He carries in his hand an open scroll. This scroll contrasts with that given the Lamb (5:1-7), which was sealed.

❏ *Revelation 10:3-4.* The prophet describes the angel's voice as "like the roar of a lion" (10:3). Perhaps John remembered the angel's voice as frightening, resonant, loud, and commanding. These ideas seem appropriate because the angel's command summons the seven thunders (10:4). These thunders stand for the voice of heaven (John 12:28-29). Notice that the seven thunders do not just make noise. They speak with understandable voices. John is about to write down what they have said when he is commanded not to do so. This command comes from yet a third source, "a voice from heaven" (10:4).

❏ *Revelation 10:5-7.* Why is the prophet told not to write down what the seven thunders have said? One answer lies in the vow taken by the colossal angel. The "mystery of God" (10:7) is about to be fulfilled in the action of the vision soon to follow. The prophet has no time to write the message of the seven thunders. Instead, the "mystery" will be played out on the stage of heaven and earth before his eyes with "no more delay" (10:6).

Yet prophecies must be written to be studied. John was commanded at the beginning of his vision and indeed throughout his prophetic experience to write down what he heard and saw (1:11, 19; 14:13; 19:9; 21:5). Why then is John specifically commanded not to write down the commands coming from the "seven thunders"? The careful reader of Revelation will note that the direct speech of God is never quoted by John. Angels and others speak for God. Jesus Christ speaks and is quoted, but not God.

The scene appears to be this: A mighty angel, colossal in size, appearance, and voice, comes to tower over earth and sea. There he is commanded by God, speaking as a voice from heaven like seven thunders, to set in motion the events that will reveal the mystery of God that has been announced to the prophets through the ages. This command is so serious that the events fulfilling the prophecies will begin without delay. Obviously then, this is a bit of a play on the reader's mind that increases the sense of mystery. The reader will "see" what is revealed but is not allowed to "hear" what God commands.

❏ *Revelation 10:8-11.* This scroll is a kind of living parable for John. He is writing a prophecy. The prophet's vocation, then, is being examined and commented on in the scene being played out. A delightful bit of inventiveness has, in one part of this story, the prophet being told not to do what prophets are called to do (write down the message given them from God);

then, in the next part of the story, the prophet is required to eat the product of his calling.

Revelation 10 and 11 are about the task and guild of the prophets, from Moses to John of Patmos. The meaning of "eating the scroll" is obvious: There could be little "sweeter" experience than hearing and seeing the Word of God, as is happening throughout this recorded vision of John. But the sweetness of this divine experience turns sour when the next part of the prophet's vocation is carried out: Tell of God's *awe*ful judgment upon the world.

❑ *Revelation 11:1-3.* While the task of "measuring" the temple may seem a bit strange, it is actually a common theme in prophetic literature. This scene (11:1-3) anticipates a more complete description of the new Jerusalem, including its measure, in Revelation 21:15-21. (Both of these passages are modeled after Ezekiel 41 and perhaps also Zechariah 2:1-5.)

Why does measuring carry importance? *Measure* means to "describe fully." Therefore, measuring the temple is a way of assuring the faithful that the promise that God will call the martyrs to "serve him day and night in his temple" (7:15) will be fulfilled. This assurance is needed because matters on earth are going to get worse very quickly.

The references to time are not as mysterious as they first appear. Forty-two months and 1,260 days both are three years and a half. The figure three and a half was made famous by its use in Daniel 7:25 and 12:7. Symbolically, three and a half is one half of seven (a number often used for completeness); therefore, its use suggests that the fulfillment of God's plan is not yet complete.

❑ *Revelation 11:4-6.* In the previous section brief mention was made of the two witnesses. They are more closely identified as "prophets" (11:10) and here are described as "olive trees" and "lampstands" (11:4). These images come directly from Zechariah 4. While the identity of these two prophets has been disputed for centuries, the description is closest to Elijah and Moses. In 1 Kings 17:1-7, Elijah causes a drought; and in Exodus 7:14-21, Moses is given power to command the plague of water turned to blood. The popular figures of Moses and Elijah (certainly the two greatest prophets of the Hebrew

Scriptures) here represent all God's prophets, including those serving the seven churches of Asia.

❑ *Revelation 11:7-10.* If these are the prophets of God in all times and places, then the ceasing of their prophecy is a sign of the end. Notice that their work is described as "testimony" (11:7). The concept of witness and testimony is critical to understanding the message of Revelation. The work of the prophets is that of making clear the presence of God in the real world. This is what makes prophets so unpopular. They keep God's message from being impoverished by enshrining it in the mere trappings of religious institutions. When prophets speak, God is conveying a message for today. Because God's thinking is not our thinking, the message for the moment— when it comes—is almost always received with hostility. If God did not protect the prophets, their kind would disappear from the earth.

In this passage the beast from the bottomless pit (modeled after the scene narrated in 9:1-6) is permitted to kill the prophets. Their deaths take place in Jerusalem ("where also their Lord was crucified" [11:8]). Because of its bloody role the city is called "Sodom" (a place of death [Isaiah 1:9]) and "Egypt" (another frequent symbol in Scripture for cruel oppression). The inhabitants of earth view the bodies with joy because prophets through the ages have been God's vocal conscience in all matters, especially in warning the rich and powerful about their arrogant oppression of widows, orphans, and all the impoverished.

History has often demonstrated that "the pen is more powerful than the sword." For this reason, those who oppress others view the work of the prophets as torment (11:10). It also explains why the words of the prophets are conveyed by the image of consuming fire from their mouths (11:5). The good news of God is always bad news for those who extort and oppress.

❑ *Revelation 11:11-13.* The bodies of the prophets suffer indignities for a brief, transitory period of earth time ("three and a half days" [11:9, 11]) and then are vindicated by God. This vindication takes the same form as that of Jesus of Nazareth, who was raised from the dead on the third day and was taken to dwell with God. The resurrection of Jesus was no mere magical resuscitation—the miraculous revival of a person thought to be dead—but a divine renewal of life of a new quality. Jesus and the martyred prophets live on high with God—the most joyous existence imaginable.

❑ **Revelation 11:14.** We are reminded by the numbering of woes that most of Chapters 10 and 11 are an interlude between the sounding of the sixth and seventh trumpets. The reference in this verse to the first and second woes connects with 9:12. Actually, what constitutes the third woe (the seventh trumpet) is rather unclear. We can probably assume that this woe should include only the material in the next few chapters that describes plagues such as we have already seen in the previous "trumpet" sections. The majority of Revelation 15, 16, and 17 is quite similar, narrating a series of plagues. The vision described in Revelation 12, 13, and 14 is of a different character. Chapters 12, 13, and 14 give the content of the "bitter-sweet" message of the little scroll.

❑ **Revelation 11:15-18.** The voices of heaven proclaim, in timeless and elegant language, the triumph of God's rule over the earthly rule of nations and kings (11:15). While the language is extraordinary, these verses also form a logical link with the chapters that follow. From this time forward, much of the action in the vision will concern the attempt of Satan and the powers of evil to defeat Christ and his kingdom of priests. At the beginning of this conflict, the victory of Christ is proclaimed. The outcome is known because God is ruler of the universe.

We are now told that the twenty-four elders also sit on thrones (11:16). This verse gives the first hint that the powers of final judgment will be shared by God with others (20:4a). The elders' proclamation of praise is based on the near approach of God taking power to judge the nations who have tormented and killed the faithful.

❑ **Revelation 11:19.** The ark of the covenant is introduced here and is never mentioned again. We can assume that the ark no longer exists in the new Jerusalem, since there is no temple there.

DIMENSION THREE:
WHAT DOES THE BIBLE MEAN TO ME?

Revelation 10

The prophet John was told that a great part of his task would be sweet. This part was like honey in his mouth. The joy of seeing heaven opened and the pleasure of being in God's presence must have been sweet. The rest of John's task was to be bitter. He had to stand up against the most powerful nation ever known to the Western world, the mighty Roman Empire.

How can this living parable of the bittersweet scroll offer insight into your life? Are you called on to perform tasks that are sweet in some aspects but bitter in others? What about the meaningful experiences of life, such as marriage, death, divorce, childbirth, helping children leave home, career changes? Is there a bittersweet quality to any of these for you? Is the church called to speak and act in ways that leave us with a bittersweet result?

Revelation 11

By its very definition, prophecy will be rejected by the majority. The New Testament prophets thought they spoke for Christ. Because Christ was rejected by the majority when he spoke, it comes as no surprise that the prophets were rejected. Evil will always "gloat over them and will celebrate by sending each other gifts" (11:10) when it no longer has to be reminded that it is evil.

Many persons believe that God continues to send us prophets. These prophets are seldom recognized for who they are while they are alive. Often they are beaten, imprisoned, and killed. What do you think about this claim? Does God still send prophets? If so, how do we know the real from the false prophets? How do you feel about the role of prophets in the church and in society? Millions of Christians throughout the world believe that Martin Luther King, Jr., was a prophet. What are the aspects of his mission that support the idea that he was? What do you think a prophet would say to you?

*This calls for patient endurance and faithfulness on
the part of the saints (13:10c).*

—— 7 ——
*The Woman Clothed
With the Sun*
Revelation 12–13

DIMENSION ONE:
WHAT DOES THE BIBLE SAY?

Answer these questions by reading Revelation 12

1. What is the first sign seen by John? (12:1)

2. What is the woman's condition? (12:2)

3. What is the second sign John sees? (12:3)

4. What does the dragon want to do? (12:4b)

5. What happens to the child? (12:5)

6. What happens to the woman clothed with the sun? (12:6)

7. What does John describe next? (12:7-9)

8. What is the good news and the bad news resulting from this event? (12:10-12)

9. When the story of the dragon and the woman clothed with the sun resumes, what new information are we given? (12:13-16)

10. How does the dragon respond to his failure? (12:17)

Answer these questions by reading Revelation 13

11. How is the "beast coming out of the sea" different from the dragon? (13:1)

12. What is the relationship between the dragon and this beast? (13:2b)

13. Which part of this new beast does John carefully describe? (13:3a)

14. How do human beings on earth respond to the beast? (13:3b-4)

15. What does this beast do and for how long? (13:5-7)

16. Who succeed in not being taken in by the beast? (13:8)

17. How are the hearers asked to respond? (13:9-10)

18. What appears next? (13:11)

19. What is this beast's relationship to the beast described earlier in this chapter? (13:12)

20. What methods does the second beast use? (13:13-17)

21. What is the number of the beast? (13:18)

DIMENSION TWO:
WHAT DOES THE BIBLE MEAN?

❏ *Revelation 12:1-2.* The literature of the ancient world (Babylonian, Persian, Greek, and Egyptian) is filled with traditions concerning pregnant, and usually divine, women who bear saviors that threaten existing gods. The identity of the woman here, however, does not depend on these stories. Rather, the imagery of Israel as a mother-nation in the Old Testament determines the meaning. Often Israel appears as a woman in the final, painful stages of childbirth (Isaiah 26:17; 66:7; Jeremiah 4:31; 13:21; 22:23; Micah 4:10; and others).

We have seen earlier that the number *twelve* links the people of God with the founding of Israel (7:1-8; 21:12-21). The sun and moon attend Israel, who is wearing "a crown of twelve stars," in giving birth to the Messiah.

❏ *Revelation 12:3.* We learn later (12:9) that this dragon is really Satan. The description of evil as a dragon is a familiar one, as a brief glance at Isaiah 27:1 and Daniel 7:7, 24-25 will show. The number of crowned heads (symbolizing authority and power) and horns is taken from the description in Daniel. The seven crowns seem to symbolize the full sovereignty of Satan on earth. Satan does have complete authority—but only on earth and only temporarily. John is careful to affirm that Christ possesses "many" crowns (19:12) and therefore will eventually conquer Satan. However, much of the detail of these two chapters depends on the chilling realization that Satan really does have massive power and authority on earth.

❏ *Revelation 12:4a.* Satan even threatens heaven. In fact, this story may hint of an early conflict in heaven in which Satan was able to destroy a significant number ("a third of the stars out of the sky" [12:4]) of God's angels. The similarity of language ("flung them to the earth" [12:4, 9]) between this reference and the more completely narrated story to follow (12:7-9) encourages us to see two separate battles.

❏ *Revelation 12:4b-5.* The child that the woman brings forth is the Christ, Jesus of Nazareth. The Gospels also speak about the vicious attacks of Satan described here. In this sense Revelation and the four Gospels agree. Satan tried in every way possible to divert Jesus from his mission and thereby to subvert God's redemption of humankind.

The faint echoes of messianic hope contained in the words "rule all the nations with an iron scepter" (see Psalm 2:9) strengthen the conclusion that the woman is Israel. The total rule of Jesus Christ will come in the final victory over evil, portrayed in Revelation 19:20. The resurrection and ascension of Jesus is described here as a rescue. The child is snatched from the clutches of Satan and taken to be with God, where we have often seen him in Revelation.

❏ *Revelation 12:6.* Israel, or the church, is literally in the desert. John refers to the destruction of the Temple and of Jerusalem in 11:1-2. Here is yet another reflection of the fugitive life of the church and Israel in the first century, following the destruction of Jerusalem in A.D. 70. God has often kept alive the hope of salvation by returning the people of God to the wilderness. I remember the wandering of Abraham, the forty-year journey of the Hebrews following their escape from Egypt, the flight of the Holy Family, and the forty-day testing of Jesus.

The 1,260 days is equivalent to the "time, times and half a time" of 12:14 and the "forty-two months" of 13:5. For the time appointed, those who dwell on earth—both the just and the unjust—will face conflict, testing, and deceit.

❏ *Revelation 12:7-9.* As we read in the opening summary of these two chapters, the story of the woman and Satan will continue with the details of her escape (12:13-17). Why does John add this interruption, telling of yet another battle in heaven? The best solution seems to be that after Christ had been raised by God and brought to heaven to reign there with God, Satan, drunk with his own power and hate, foolishly stormed heaven in pursuit of the Christ. The thrilling account of what took place has excited the imagination of artists and storytellers for centuries. You will notice that this story of angelic battle has a distinct Old Testament flavor, even though such a story is not even hinted at elsewhere in Scripture. Still, the angel Michael is a prominent figure, especially in Daniel (10:13, 21; 12:1). The result of Michael's victory is that Satan is expelled from the heavenly regions. Satan returns to earth with his angels.

❏ *Revelation 12:10-12.* The beginnings of final and complete salvation are seen in the exile of Satan. He is described in 12:10 as "the accuser," that is, the one who constantly misrepresents the faithful of earth in the presence of God. If angels mediate for the welfare of God's people, Satan mediates for their harm. The situation of the faithful is still hazardous. The saints only conquer when they appeal to the salvation won by Christ as the crucified lamb of the Passover.

❏ *Revelation 12:13-17.* The flight of the woman to the wilderness may be modeled on the story of Elijah fleeing the wrath of Jezebel (1 Kings 19:4-8). Or John may have used the wilderness experience of Jesus, when he was tempted for forty days in the desert (Matthew 4:1-11; Mark 1:12-13; Luke 4:1-13), as his model. In both cases, as well as that of the Hebrews wandering in the wilderness for forty years following their deliverance from Egypt, God miraculously nourished and sustained the pilgrims (Revelation 12:6). The image of being borne by an eagle's wings is very powerful. Flight, especially effortless flight, has been the welcomed image of freedom in times of oppression. The mere sight of a soaring bird has often given captives strength to stay alive.

Satan's anger now turns on the rest of the woman's children, the faithful followers of Christ who remain on earth. Satan's anger is doubled. Not only did he fail in destroying the Son of God and was defeated in heaven when he pursued him there, he also was unsuccessful when he sought to destroy the child's mother. The children of God will now face the full wrath of Satan.

❏ *Revelation 13:1-4.* The first beast comes from the sea. The connection between the sea and monsters representing danger and chaos is often made in the Old Testament, especially by Ezekiel (Ezekiel 29:3; 32:2). Also read Daniel 7:3-7.

In this passage the head mortally wounded but now healed represented for John a person parading as divine whose wound, now healed, was a cheap imitation of Christ's death and resurrection. Perhaps John understood this "head" to be the Roman emperor Nero, who was worshiped as a god, committed suicide, and was rumored to be still alive. The goal of the beast from the sea is to displace God and the Lamb as a worthy object of worship. To discredit this portrayal as too fantastic to be credible would be a mistake. This counterfeit deity is genuinely powerful, awesome, and convincing.

❑ *Revelation 13:5-10.* The beast can "exercise his authority for forty-two months." To resist the beast requires faith and endurance. Why does John concentrate on the blasphemy of this false Christ? Blasphemy is using the name of God wrongly. We may think of this as cursing, but a more basic meaning is "claiming to be God." If God is to remain God, then anyone or anything claiming to be God is blasphemy. The beast's chief instrument of deceit has the same effect as idolatry, demeaning God to become God.

❑ *Revelation 13:11-17.* A second beast who serves the first beast arises out of the earth. Revelation's favorite name for the Christ is "the Lamb" (13:8). The beast from the earth appears "like a lamb" but speaks "like a dragon" (13:11). These acts are consistent with how Satan works, by a sly and convincing parody of what is true and genuine. If evil were easy to identify, it would not be nearly as successful as it is. The lamb-dragon carries out the sea beast's deceit and, in fact, functions under his authority.

The most terrifying of the techniques of the second beast is no mere magical trick but a cruel use of economics. To eat, one must worship the beast by receiving its mark. Even the rich cannot buy exemption from the mark of the beast.

The means of identification used by the forces of evil is an imitation of God's salvation. The 144,000 of the new Israel also were sealed on the forehead (7:3). As a final irony John deftly points out that those who compromise themselves by accepting the mark of the beast do not even worship the real beast; they worship an image of the beast. The nations of earth have been doubly deceived.

❑ *Revelation 13:18.* The number 666 is meant by John to be understandable to his readers. Exactly who John had in mind is now lost to us; but almost certainly the number refers to the cruel emperor of Rome, Nero. On another level this mysterious number is the name of that willingness in all of us to displace God with a god of our own making.

THE WOMAN CLOTHED WITH THE SUN   **55**

DIMENSION THREE:
WHAT DOES THE BIBLE MEAN TO ME?

Revelation 12

How can we lift our sights beyond the traditional view of the devil as a dragon? What is the problem with this view of Satan? How do you think the devil makes evil most apparent today?

The Bible claims that God and God's angels have already spelled the defeat of Satan. Do you think that the devil's days are numbered? If so, what signs might signal this event?

Can you think of any examples in which God has rescued "the saints" from danger? If so, what are they? What would be the modern equivalent of "water like a river" (12:15) seeking to destroy God's people?

Revelation 13

How are negative and destructive forces disguised as good? If evil convinces by imitating goodness, how does one identify evil without doing harm to innocent people?

What kind of authority (economic, political, or social) is most dangerous in our world and society today? Revelation 13:5-11 suggests that the devil will defeat some Christians. How does Satan conquer Christians today?

False prophets use trickery to convince people that the religion they promote is true. What gimmicks do modern false prophets use? Who are those who suffer today because of economic systems and problems?

They were purchased from among men
and offered as firstfruits to God and the Lamb (14:4c).

—— 8 ——
Singing a New Song
Revelation 14–15

DIMENSION ONE:
WHAT DOES THE BIBLE SAY?

Answer these questions by reading Revelation 14

1. What do the 144,000 have inscribed on their foreheads? (14:1)

2. How did the voice from heaven sound? (14:2)

3. Who is allowed to learn the new song? (14:3)

4. How many different ways are the 144,000 described? (14:4-5)

5. What does the first angel say to all the earth's people? (14:7)

6. What is the second angel's message? (14:8)

7. What does the third angel announce? (14:9-11)

8. Who is pronounced blessed by the Spirit? (14:13)

9. Who appears on a white cloud, and how is he described? (14:14)

10. What does the "one, 'like a son of man' " do with his sickle? (14:15-16)

11. Who else has a sharp sickle? (14:17)

12. Who is the last angel described in this scene? (14:18)

13. What does this angel do? (14:18)

14. Where is the winepress of God located? (14:20)

15. What does the winepress produce? (14:20)

DIMENSION TWO:
WHAT DOES THE BIBLE MEAN?

❑ *Revelation 14:1.* While the metaphors and images of Revelation are rich and powerful, we see in this chapter several examples of the elusive character of its style. Many elements of this chapter refer to people, places, and scenes we viewed earlier. Others point to passages that will narrate in more detail events to come. Throughout this chapter the strength and beauty of the vision itself is what counts. This strength and beauty will be greatly diminished if we try to make the vision neat and tidy by putting it in an ironclad framework of time and space.

The 144,000 is the group spoken of in 7:1-8. This number represents the fullness of God's redeemed people throughout history. *Mount Zion* is another name for Jerusalem and, more specifically, always suggests the site of the Temple. The reference to "his Father's name" reminds us of the burning bush story in Exodus 3. There, God reveals the holy name as "I AM WHO I AM" (Exodus 3:14).

❑ *Revelation 14:2-3.* John is often at a loss to find words equal to what he saw and heard. When he says the voice was like rushing water, rolling thunder, and a gigantic choir of harps, he means the sound was unlike any he had ever heard. I would like to hear how a brilliant musical composer with unlimited resources might interpret such a sound.

❑ *Revelation 14:4-5.* We are given a full picture of the redeemed for the first time. The emphasis in this description is on purity. This emphasis should come as no surprise in light of the seven letters to the churches. They reveal that the widespread and morally corrupt religions of the Roman Empire were a constant threat to Christians. The list of sins in 9:20-21 demonstrates that sexual immorality was closely connected with the idolatrous practices of many of these cults. Describing the redeemed as chaste virgins who are morally unblemished (spotless) is one idea, not two. Moral purity, for Christians of the Roman Empire, necessarily concerned the dual issues of idolatry and sexual practices. Not lying, in light of the threat of martyrdom, may specifically refer to not denying that Christ is Lord and God is Creator, even under threat of torture and death.

❑ *Revelation 14:6-7.* Before beginning a litany of awesome judgments, we are given an interlude for the praise of God. This call to praise is good news to all inhabitants of the earth. When those who have been created give praise to the Creator of all things, they find in their praise the most intimate reason for life. Because God the Creator is sovereign over all things, it is good news, not bad news, when the hour of judgment comes.

John also uses a subtle play on words here. The call is to *worship* the Creator. Those who do worship God have nothing to be anxious about in the coming judgment. But in 14:9-11, a frightening reward is anticipated for those who *worship* the creature. This contrast reminds readers of how this creature leads humans astray. The creature claims to be the Creator, demanding acts of worship that belong only to the true God of creation.

❑ *Revelation 14:8.* We will hear a great deal more about Babylon in Chapters 17 and 18. The female figure is described here as the priestess of an intoxicating passion. The exact meaning of the metaphor is a bit more complex than may first appear. Revelation 17:6 identifies the wine she offers as the "blood of the saints." Her status as a prostitute is also emphasized (17:5), so her passion could also be a part of the symbolic wine. The full description of Babylon's fall must wait for our study of Revelation 17–18.

❑ *Revelation 14:9-11.* We have just come from a vivid portrayal of the worshipers of a false god (13:11-17), and now we learn of their reward. The imagery used by John is a play on Babylon's "maddening wine of her adulteries" (14:8). God's wine of wrath will have to be endured in continual torment by those who drink from Babylon's cup. (This play on images is somewhat disguised by the New International Version. The word *maddening* in 14:8 is the same Greek word translated "wrath" in 14:10.)

In the Old Testament, God's wrath of judgment is often described as a pouring out as from a cup (Isaiah 51:17; 63:6; Jeremiah 10:25; 42:18; Ezekiel 7:8; Hosea 5:10; Habakkuk 2:15). The image of God's wrath as wine in a cup is found in Jeremiah 25:15. But the wine of God's wrath is not yet poured out. Rather, the cup of God's anger is filled (Revelation 14:10). The pouring out will take place with the seven bowls of wrath, described in Revelation 16.

❏ *Revelation 14:12-13.* The rhythm of Revelation is maintained here. The encouragement of the faithful is contrasted with their desperate circumstances. They are constantly being threatened with oppression and death because of their loyalty to Christ. The only solution to the present circumstance of oppression is "patient endurance." Endurance is not mere survival. The goal of survival would require impossible moral compromises. Rather, endurance arises out of total dedication to God's laws and faithfulness to Jesus.

Following the Lamb "wherever he goes" (14:4b) means following the Redeemer in the service of healing, personal suffering, and perhaps sacrificial death. Those who die while persisting in goodness and fidelity will be blessed. The Spirit gives this benediction, suggesting that the final confirmation comes from the life-giving source of creation. The Spirit was the vehicle of creation in the beginning, and the Spirit gives life in the present.

❏ *Revelation 14:14-16.* A popular portrayal of death suggests that "the grim reaper" is a kind of supernatural being in a secular group of gods. Here, Jesus as Son of man is set in the role of returning Judge of the nations. Jesus appeared this way in the midst of the churches of Asia (1:13), and he will appear in this way in final judgment.

The harvest is called for by an angel ambassador from God's temple in heaven. This picture is a reminder that even the

Christ does not know the hour. Like all others, he must await the command of God to begin the time of judgment.

❏ *Revelation 14:17-18.* That Jesus, the Son of man, will be assisted by saints and angels in the work of judging the nations is a theme that strengthens a conviction even more basic than the act of judgment itself. The goal of the Final Judgment is to establish the kingdom of God as the dominant reality of existence for all people. God does not judge to show divine authority but to perfect the people of God.

The purpose of the people of God is to praise God. In this way the viewpoint of Revelation is that God's judgment is the perfection of praise. Without judgment as a climactic act in history, a new era of the kingdom of God cannot begin. The goal of the renewed Kingdom is to establish the praise of God as the central reality of life.

John relies heavily on Old Testament images in Chapter 14. The angel "who had charge of the fire" is an excellent example. In the Temple sacrificial system even the fire on the altar was sacred. Only the priests were permitted to kindle the first fire (Leviticus 1:7). Moreover, fire symbolized the presence of God. In the prophetic writings of the Old Testament, the most common image of God's wrath is fire. Thus, "the angel, who had charge of the fire" is the one with authority to take wrath from God's altar. Mixing *fire* with *harvest* may seem an inappropriate mingling of symbols, but the power of the vision requires this piling up of images. This powerful vision conveys the seriousness and power of God's judgment.

❏ *Revelation 14:19-20.* Perhaps no stimulus to the imagination in Revelation is better known than this fascinating vision. The second line of "The Battle Hymn of the Republic" is drawn from this passage ("He is trampling out the vintage where the grapes of wrath are stored.").

Another captivating metaphor is also seen here. The description of blood flowing as high as a horse's bridle leaves us speechless—because of the suffering it suggests and the artistry with which it is suggested.

❏ *Conclusion.* Many people who have never read Revelation carefully assume that this book is one long, uninterrupted account of disaster and judgment. This is not true, as you have learned. Revelation has more good news than bad news, destruction, and mayhem.

The prophet John wisely scattered throughout this book pockets of calm, soothing moments in the presence of God. Chapter 14 is one of these pockets of calm. Christians have learned anew in each generation that the inner peace and calm learned by praising God can defeat the rage and chaos created by forces of evil oppression. In this chapter we have seen that endurance is the key to the possibility of persecuted Christians surviving under incredible suffering and temptation.

DIMENSION THREE:
WHAT DOES THE BIBLE MEAN TO ME?

Revelation 14:1-5

When you think of a perfect life, how does it appear to you? Sit quietly and reflect for a few moments. Should life in heaven be totally different than life on earth? Or, would you want most of what you find good about life here and now made better or perfected? What does *being redeemed* mean? How can you know that you are redeemed? Is it a good idea to seek such knowledge?

Revelation 14:6-7

Do you find that the praise of God brings you closer to the center of who you are? What does it mean to praise God? Is the praise of God always with spoken words? How can your life and work be praise? How does the knowledge that God created and controls the universe sustain and strengthen you?

Revelation 14:8-11

Do you believe that evil exists in the world? How are people and nations led astray? Revelation was written in difficult times. How is the present difficult and critical, even though we do not always see it? Do you share the belief that God will punish those who follow false gods? If so, how do you justify this belief in light of the world's desire for a God who cares for all people and saves them? Is the goal of God's creation and salvation the redemption of all people?

Revelation 14:12-13

Patient endurance characterized the life of Jesus. Frequently, the Bible calls us to be persistent. If endurance is tolerant of delay in seeing justice accomplished, then how will the world ever be changed for the better? How would you describe the best kind of endurance? How can endurance keep from being cowardly passivity or hypocritical apathy? How is survival something different from endurance?

Revelation 14:14-20

Does it concern you that the Book of Revelation proclaims Jesus as the coming Judge of the nations? How does your understanding of Jesus conflict with his portrayal as "son of man" in this passage? How do you reconcile God's wrath with the good news of salvation?

Go, pour out the seven bowls of God's wrath
on the earth (16:1).

9

Seven Bowls of Wrath
Revelation 15–16

DIMENSION ONE:
WHAT DOES THE BIBLE SAY?

Answer these questions by reading Revelation 15

1. What was the sign John the prophet saw in heaven? (15:1)

2. Who stands beside the sea of glass? (15:2a)

3. What are they doing? (15:2b-3)

4. What does the song foresee? (15:4c)

5. Where do the angels with the plagues come from? (15:5-6)

6. Who gives the angels the golden bowls full of wrath? (15:7)

7. What happens in the temple after this? (15:8)

Answer these questions by reading Revelation 16

8. What is the first plague poured out of the golden bowl by the angel? (16:2)

9. What is the second plague poured out? (16:3)

10. How is the third plague like the second? (16:4)

11. How are the two plagues of blood infecting water explained? (16:5-7)

12. What is the fourth plague? (16:8)

13. Whom do the humans (followers of the beast) blame for the plagues? (16:9)

14. Against what is the fifth plague directed? (16:10)

15. What is the result of this plague? (16:10-11)

16. On what does the sixth plague fall? (16:12)

17. Why is the river dried up? (16:12)

18. How do the dragon, the beast, and the false prophet respond to this plague? (16:13-14)

19. Where is the final battle to be held? (16:16)

20. What takes place when the seventh golden bowl is poured out? (16:18-21)

21. Who is particularly singled out for destruction? (16:19)

DIMENSION TWO:
WHAT DOES THE BIBLE MEAN?

❑ *Revelation 15:1.* Revelation 9:12 and 11:14 mention three woes, but only two woes are described. Possibly, the seven bowls of plagues described in Chapters 15 and 16 make up the third woe. Many of these plagues are similar to events that follow the blowing of the seven trumpets (Revelation 8 and 9)—with one difference. Now the wrath of God is brought to fulfillment. The trumpet disasters limited destruction to one third; now total destruction is described.

❑ *Revelation 15:2-4.* Once again the heavenly company of saints who have victoriously endured the deceits of the beast are seen in the midst of their adoration of God. The hymn they sing has a distinguished heritage. It contains elements of the song composed by Moses (Exodus 15:1-18) and of a song composed by Jesus Christ in praise of God. This hymn has a majestic and familiar tone to it; but the exact text, as reported here, is found nowhere else. The words extol the fairness and power of God. The hymn is quite universal in scope, describing God as Lord of all the nations and the eventual participation of the people of earth in the praise of God.

❑ *Revelation 15:5-7.* The seven golden bowls filled with plagues is the last "seven series" we will meet in Revelation. The plagues have a certain finality about them, both in what they contain and in what they hint at to take place later on. The source of power in this passage is the temple of God in heaven. The seven bowls are filled with God's wrath, and the result of their being poured out will foreshadow the end.

❑ *Revelation 15:8.* The temple being filled with smoke is the result of an unusually strong manifestation of God's glory. The idea of smoke or other natural phenomena being present when God visits a place is merely an attempt to symbolize the effect God's presence has. In Old Testament usage God's glory is essentially the same as God's presence. When God is present, no human can stand. Moses had this experience (Exodus 40:35): "Moses could not enter the Tent of Meeting because the cloud had settled upon it, and the glory of the LORD filled the tabernacle." Ezekiel's experience was similar: "The cloud filled the temple, and the court was full of the radiance of the glory of the LORD" (Ezekiel 10:4b).

This display of divine power clears the temple and creates an atmosphere of dread and expectancy. The unfolding of events has taken on a fresh and frightening dimension.

❑ *Revelation 16:1-2.* In Revelation 13:16-17, those who worship the image of the beast and receive its mark are allowed to prosper for a time. With the first plague, the days of temporary prosperity are over for them. This theme is classic in the Bible. God may allow evil to have its temporal power and success for a time, but a powerful reversal will come in the moment of divine judgment. This theme of reversal is perhaps the most distinctive feature of all New Testament eschatology (accounts of the end of time).

The plague described here is similar to the plague brought by God through Moses against the Egyptians (Exodus 9:10-11). The two adjectives used to describe the sores might be translated in modern language as "gross and disgusting."

❑ *Revelation 16:3.* The second plague is parallel to the second trumpet (8:8-9), with the difference that now all the sea and its inhabitants are destroyed. This plague is similar to the first plague against the Egyptians (Exodus 7:17-21).

❑ *Revelation 16:4.* As in the third trumpet (8:10-11), destruction of fresh water follows that of salt water. The same means of destruction is described: The water is turned to blood. The use of blood is explained in the verses that follow and is an ironic image based on the principle of "Let the punishment fit the crime."

❑ *Revelation 16:5-7.* We are building up quite a list of angels who are in charge of various things. We have met the angels with power over the winds (7:1), the angel with power over fire (14:18), and now the angel in charge of the waters. This angel sings a song of praise to God. The song is a justification of the divine justice apparent in this plague.

❑ *Revelation 16:8-9.* The effect of the fourth trumpet (8:12) is to diminish the heat and light of the sun, moon, and stars. In an interesting reversal the sun's power is heightened here to bring the torment of unbearable heat. In a scientific age we now know how just a little shift in weather patterns can bring devastation to life on earth.

❑ *Revelation 16:10-11.* For the first time in Revelation the beast receives the direct power of God's wrath. The plague of darkness is like another plague against the Egyptians (Exodus 10:21-23).

For the first time the beast is described as having a kingdom. The darkness is a threat to its kingdom because the darkness suggests a limit to the beast's power and authority. If the beast were divine, it could control light and darkness.

At the conclusion of the fourth and fifth plagues, the followers of the beast do not repent. They curse God as the cause of their punishment. This theme occurs throughout Scripture. When suffering a just punishment for sins of our own making, we are strongly tempted to blame God's justice rather than our lack of justice. The message of the prophets in response is quite consistent. If you act and speak in a way that clearly is in conflict with the divine mandate of God, do not blame God for the outcome. Perhaps the most vivid pronouncement of this prophetic principle is Ezekiel's oracle concerning sour grapes (Ezekiel 18).

❑ *Revelation 16:12.* When the angel blew the sixth trumpet (9:13-19), the armies at the Euphrates were released. The sixth bowl spilled out creates the same effect. The Euphrates is dried up, allowing free access to the eastern kingdoms. The Roman Empire lived in fear of these kingdoms, and this military strategy would have been immediately understandable to well-informed Roman citizens.

❑ *Revelation 16:13-16.* The dragon and the beast, acting in concert, devise a plan that plays right into the final strategy of God's judgment. They send deceiving spirits to convince the nations to meet God in battle. (The conclusion of the story of Armageddon will be delayed until 20:7-10.) These acts may seem a ridiculous display of foolhardiness. However, John's purpose is to tell a kind of parable about the character of idolatry, not to portray logical and reasonable actions.

The strategy of the beasts here is a word picture of idolatry deceiving itself to the end of self-destruction. The danger is to make it into an otherworldly fantasy tale involving creatures beyond our wildest imaginations. The fact is that this process of self-deception leading to destruction is exactly that of human sin and something we all do.

❏ *Revelation 16:17-21.* Earthquakes were common and greatly feared in Asia Minor (Turkey), and archaeological research adds new information every decade to our growing understanding of the devastation created by earthquakes throughout history. Revelation often speaks of earthquakes as a means of God's punishment (6:12; 8:5; 11:13, 19).

Babylon is almost certainly the city of Rome. John uses yet another delightful but macabre play on images in 16:19. Babylon has given the wine of her cup to the nations (14:8); but now God will force her to empty, to the last drop, the divine cup of fury.

DIMENSION THREE:
WHAT DOES THE BIBLE MEAN TO ME?

Revelation 15:3-4

Why do you worship God? Do you know why some people you know do not claim to worship God? The hope expressed in the beautiful hymn of Revelation 15:3-4 is that the entire world will one day see the justice of God's judgments and come to worship God. What do you think keeps people from acknowledging the universal sovereignty of God?

Revelation 15:5-8

When God's glory fills a space, no human can stand to be in that same space. If these events are true in the Bible, why does no one seem to testify to such awesome experiences today? Where and how do you think God is present in power today?

Revelation 16:1-11

Both here and in the Exodus account of the plagues, people who receive God's judgment in the form of horrible punishments do not seem to recognize their responsibility for the outcome of their sins. Rather, they blame God for their troubles. Why do people react this way? Does this description correspond to how you think people behave? Why did the people of God always reject the words of the prophet? Why do we?

Revelation 16:12-14

What makes anyone—whether strange cosmic beings such as those described here or humans—think they can "be God" and live as though nothing can keep them from succeeding? What are some examples of ways that people "play God"? How are they found out? Are we always doomed to failure when we try to do this?

Revelation 16:15

These words were written about 1900 years ago. They were written as if spoken by Christ to those who read this book. What does it mean today to stay vigilant while waiting for the perfection of God's rule?

I will explain to you the mystery of the woman (17:7).

10
Babylon Is Fallen
Revelation 17–18

DIMENSION ONE:
WHAT DOES THE BIBLE SAY?

Answer these questions by reading Revelation 17

1. Who is the woman who sits on many waters? (17:1)

2. What is the charge against her? (17:2)

3. Where is the woman next seated? (17:3)

4. What does she hold in her hand? (17:4)

5. What is her name, and how do we know it? (17:5)

6. Who interprets the meaning of the mystery to John? (17:7)

7. According to the angel, how are the following parts of the vision to be interpreted? (17:8-15):

The beast with seven heads and ten horns? (17:8a)

The inhabitants of the earth? (17:8b)

The seven heads on the beast? (17:9-10)

The ten horns? (17:12)

The waters on which the prostitute sits? (17:15)

8. What does the angel say will happen to the prostitute? (17:16)

9. Why will this happen? (17:17)

10. Who is this woman? (17:18)

Answer these questions by reading Revelation 18

11. What lives in Babylon, according to the angel with great authority? (18:2)

12. Who has been contaminated by Babylon? (18:3)

13. To whom does the next voice speak? (18:4)

14. Why is it important for the people to get out of Babylon? (18:4)

15. On what principle will Babylon be punished? (18:6)

16. What does Babylon think about herself? (18:7)

17. Who will weep for Babylon? (18:9)

18. Why do the merchants of the earth weep for her? (18:11-17a)

19. Why do those who earn their living from the sea weep for the destruction of the city? (18:17b-19)

20. While kings, merchants, and seafaring men weep, who is asked to rejoice? (18:20)

21. In the next action of the vision, what does the angel do? (18:21)

22. What will no longer be found in Babylon? (18:22-23)

23. What is the final reason given for Babylon's fall? (18:24)

DIMENSION TWO:
WHAT DOES THE BIBLE MEAN?

❏ *Revelation 17:1-2.* The topic of Revelation 17 and 18 is the punishment of Rome. By "great prostitute" John means "notorious prostitute." Rome's fornication is identified as the religious cults with their sets of gods. John will play on the theme of wine and drunkenness throughout these chapters.

❏ *Revelation 17:3-6a.* John carefully explains why the woman is on the scarlet beast (17:7-14). From earlier appearances, we know that the beast of the bottomless pit is Satan (9:1-2, 11; 11:7). The woman is on the beast because evil is supported by the source of evil. John is saying that Rome is an agent of the devil. He is also introducing a deliberate contrast with the woman clothed with the sun (Chapter 12). The description of the woman is based on Jeremiah 51:7, with considerable interpretation added by John.

We are meant to find this woman repugnant in every way (just as we are meant to find the woman in Chapter 12 sympathetic in every way). The final description of her drunkenness is especially revolting. She is drunk with the killing of faithful Christians.

❑ *Revelation 17:6b-14.* This passage is the only place in Revelation where John is given an extensive interpretation of what he has seen in his vision. We are grateful to John for including the interpretive guide given him; otherwise, we might be at a loss to make it out.

The most significant and difficult part of this vision concerns the beast with seven heads and ten horns. We met this strange creature in Chapters 12 and 13. Now we learn that the seven heads are seven hills (mountains). In the ancient world Rome was known as the City of Seven Hills. These seven hills, ranged along the eastern bank of the Tiber River, were named and well known throughout the Roman world. The details of which Roman emperor is which of the seven kings linked with these seven hills is not at all clear, but the general drift certainly is. The meaning of the prophecy of ten kings, represented by the ten horns (17:12), is that the kings of earth will be gathered in one final "war against the Lamb" (17:14).

❑ *Revelation 17:15-18.* The Roman Empire did sit on many waters. The excellent shipping industry and Roman naval patrols, protecting coastlines and sea routes, as much as the Roman system of roads, explained Rome's economic wealth. Yet Rome was hated by the nations and tribes it defeated and subjected. This passage looks to a time when the slave states under the dominion of Rome will rise to destroy the master. God has motivated the subjected kings to cooperate with Rome for a period. Eventually, however, the kingdoms of earth will unite behind an evil power whose only aim is to destroy the prostitute (Rome). The object is to force Satan, the beast, to show his hand. Once he does, God will destroy forever the devil's tyranny.

❑ *Revelation 18:1-3.* This pronouncement of doom reflects a sober realism in the assessment of Roman power. John knows full well what a mistake it is, out of justified rage over oppression, to underestimate the strength of one's enemies. Rome is great. But if Rome is great, so much greater will be her fall. The description in verse 2 uses a technique often found in the Old Testament prophets. John looks ahead to a time when Rome will lie in ruins and become a haven for unclean spirits and vultures. This terrible future awaits Rome because she has promoted the worship of untold numbers of false gods and has persecuted and killed faithful followers of the church.

❑ *Revelation 18:4-8.* The scene of Rome's destruction is so frightful that another voice calls out to rescue the people of God still in the city lest they be harmed as innocent bystanders. The viewpoint here is that one's environment can be dangerous. Rome is a threat to Christians for two reasons: Christians could easily get caught up in the subtle sins of the empire; and, with the coming destruction, good people might get harmed in a kind of spill-over effect.

The Old Testament principle of "an eye for an eye, a tooth for a tooth" is applied to Rome by God. But it is double jeopardy for her; she will receive double back for the evil she has done. The reason for this double punishment is her arrogance and god-playing.

❑ *Revelation 18:9-10.* John now describes a series of three groups who stand watching Rome being destroyed (kings, merchants, and seafarers). None of these groups expresses any sympathy for Rome; they merely regret the economic loss that Rome's fall means to them. The Roman Empire expanded by a slow process of military conquest; exploration of wild regions; political alliances and trade agreements; and, on rare occasions, by invitation from weak, needy countries. These people probably thought life under Rome would be preferable to constant fear of stronger enemies. Revelation is quite accurate to speak of a large number of kings in attendance at Rome's destruction. The Roman emperor at the time of Revelation's writing was master of an unknown but large number of local kings.

❏ *Revelation 18:11-17a.* Trade made Rome great. Trade was made possible by the feared legions of Rome and their constant patrol of land and sea routes. The list in verses 11-13 is, if anything, quite modest. *Scarlet* refers to an entire industry of dye production. The silk, spices, pearls, and scented woods remind us that Rome maintained a steady shipping trade with countries as far distant as India and China.

The decadent indulgences made possible by Rome's wealth are aptly described in verse 16. The abrupt end to these indulgences is just as jarringly described in verse 17: "In one hour such great wealth has been brought to ruin!"

❏ *Revelation 18:17b-19.* John's artistic portrayal of the funeral party at Rome's wake includes "all who had ships on the sea." John prophetically proclaims Rome has been laid waste and a great shipping trade on the Mediterranean has been thereby destroyed.

The point of all three of these funeral laments is that Rome had no real friends. Rome was feared and, when allowed to dominate, brought fabulous wealth that benefited some people. Rome's destruction by God brings mourning, but only because of the loss of power and wealth.

❏ *Revelation 18:20.* If kings, merchants, and seafarers mourn the destruction of Rome, many rejoice. By the list, "saints and apostles and prophets," we are meant to include all the faithful, reaching back to Abraham and Sarah, who have served God in truth under duress by the many Babylons of the ages.

❏ *Revelation 18:21-23.* This description of Babylon's condition after God's judgment has taken place is an amazing example of prophetic faith in God's word. The haunting picture of empty, still streets, buildings, and public places such as the Forum and Colosseum casts a pall across the hearer's mind.

❏ *Revelation 18:24.* The motivation of God's destruction of Rome is not based solely on the murder of Christians. "All who have been killed" recalls that millions had been killed by Rome in her need to dominate. I am glad to learn that John also is concerned for the vast numbers who were not Christians but who suffered just as cruelly.

DIMENSION THREE:
WHAT DOES THE BIBLE MEAN TO ME?

Revelation 17:1-6a, 15-18

In Revelation we have discovered that John is concerned about all humanity and the created order, not just Christians. Do you think that the great prostitute is meant to refer only to the enemies of the church? If prostitution is essentially a compromise with morality, are we all guilty, at some time in our lives, of prostitution? What do you think might be modern examples of adulterous compromises with evil?

Revelation 17:6b-14

John is concerned about the history of his world. He sees a pattern of evil and oppressive kingdoms. How do you view political history? As you reflect on what you know about history, do you think John was being overly pessimistic or cynical? Is the political history of the world and its nations as bleak as John seems to believe? What, in your opinion, are the reasons for John thinking this way? What are the standards by which we judge our history?

Revelation 18:1-18

"The bigger they are, the harder they fall" is a rather good summary of this chapter. Rome was a mighty, even glorious, empire with astounding accomplishments. John makes Rome, however, into a kind of parable about the dangers of self-deception and self-idolatry. How can this parable relate to other situations? Can it apply to individuals? How does our culture evaluate the accomplishments of nations, institutions, and individuals? What are the dangers in admiring power and wealth? How do you maintain a sense of self-esteem and self-confidence and yet avoid destructive self-worship? What signs do you see around you that might lead you to conclude that self-deception is still a problem?

Revelation 18:19-24

John's description of various groups mourning over the fall of Babylon is so vivid and compelling that it could almost be the script for a drama or movie. Put yourself in the place of these groups and imagine how you would feel about the defeat of someone on whom you are dependent but whom you also resent. What are the dynamics of such a relationship? Can you think of any modern equivalents? For example, what is it like to be dependent on the welfare of the state and have those benefits taken away? How is the picture here an accurate portrayal of mutual manipulation in all situations?

Hallelujah! Salvation and glory and power belong to our God (19:1).

—— 11 ——
The Sword of His Mouth
Revelation 19–20

DIMENSION ONE:
WHAT DOES THE BIBLE SAY?

Answer these questions by reading Revelation 19

1. Why does the multitude praise God? (19:2)

2. Who else praises God? (19:4-5)

3. What is the topic of the hymn sung to God? (19:6-8)

4. What does the angel say when John tries to worship him? (19:10)

5. What are the names given to Christ? (19:11, 13, 16)

6. What does Christ come to do? (19:11, 15)

7. To whom does the angel call, and what does he order them to do? (19:17-18)

8. Who has gathered to do battle? (19:19)

9. What happens to the beast and the false prophet? (19:20c)

10. What happens to the kings and their armies? (19:21)

Answer these questions by reading Revelation 20

11. What happens to Satan? (20:1-3)

12. During this one thousand years, what happens to those who have conquered Satan's forces? (20:4)

13. What happens to the "rest of the dead"? (20:5)

14. How does John describe those who are raised? (20:6)

15. What happens after the one thousand years? (20:7-8)

16. What happens to this huge army? (20:9)

17. What happens to Satan? (20:10)

18. What is the next event? (20:11)

19. Why has God come? (20:12-13)

20. How is this judgment done? (20:12)

21. What happens to death and Hades? (20:14)

22. Who else is thrown into the lake of fire? (20:15)

DIMENSION TWO:
WHAT DOES THE BIBLE MEAN?

❏ *Revelation 19:1-5.* We last heard a multitude praising God in Chapter 15 (verses 2-4). The resounding cry here begins with "Hallelujah!" Only by reading on in these chapters does the reason for the *hallelujah* become clear. Victory over Satan has been forecast in Revelation, but for the first time the victory is narrated.

❏ *Revelation 19:6-10.* This hymn is more than poetic language using time-honored phrases. It is really a hymn of creation. When life is brought into unity with the Creator of life, then the goal of creation has been fulfilled.

The image of this perfect union of purpose and reality is the marriage of Christ. But who is the bride? The power of the image is destroyed if we precisely define the bride. Because the bride's festive garment is the collective righteousness of the church, the bride cannot be the church. Rather, as in the Gospels, the wedding feast is a sign of the fulfillment of the kingdom of God. When the Kingdom triumphs, the groom is joined in marriage to the bride.

This frankly intimate metaphor is meant to contrast with the impure sexual intimacy offered by the drunken prostitute—the purveyor of self-love and oppression. This underplayed contrast is made obvious by the bride's dress, "righteous acts." Any and all can be Christ's bride—great and small, male and female, rich and poor. But the wedding garment is the same for all and cannot be bought. The wedding garment is the garment of pure confession. The confession is that God and the Lamb are "King of kings and Lord of lords" (19:16). *Confession* does not mean mere recitation of a creed but confession with feet and, hands and, if necessary, with one's life.

In Revelation the atmosphere in which God exists is worship. Into this very air Christians are called. As the book unfolds, we learn that *worship* is an expansive term. *Worship* includes hard work (the literal meaning of *liturgy*) and personal sacrifice.

❏ *Revelation 19:11-16.* The white horse (6:2) of conquest signals the fulfillment of Christ's victory. John carefully describes Christ. The descriptions are really titles for Christ. *Faithful* and *True* are appropriate names for the Son of God. To say that Christ is faithful suggests loyalty to someone or to a vow or principle. Jesus Christ is loyal to his people and will sustain them as their champion, whatever the situation. Jesus promised that he would return to establish the kingdom of God in its fullness. Here we see an anticipated vision of Jesus the Christ doing so. Jesus, in his earthly ministry, reached out to include all peoples in a renewed family of God. In 20:4-6, we see a remnant of this community being gathered. Jesus Christ is trustworthy to bring to perfect conclusion all that was begun in Creation. Christ is the "True" one in the sense that he is the genuine Christ, not the cheap parody as seen in the sea beast, who at best can only imitate Christ.

As we saw in Revelation 12 and 13, the false Christ wears countless crowns. We know the number (name) of the beast (666), but Christ has a name that only he knows. Therefore, no one has power over Christ. In every way Christ is a superior force to the powers of Satan.

Christ is also "the Word of God" (19:13). This title is quite rare in the New Testament. He is called the Word only here and in the Gospel of John (John 1:1, 14). We usually think of *word* as either oral speech or a written document used to convey thoughts. When the Old Testament prophets spoke, they often began, "The word of the LORD came to me, saying . . ." The New Testament also speaks about the gospel of Christ and the Kingdom as "the word of God." But here Christ is "the Word." That is, he is the revelation of God's message.

Only Jesus Christ can be the Word of God because Jesus is in such unity with God that what he does and says is God acting and speaking. What Christ does here is make war on sin and deceit. He does this by the sword of his mouth, a fascinating image perfectly suited to the presentation of Christ as "the Word of God." From the mouth of the Word comes the word that creates and that can also destroy. As the Word, the Son of God was with God at Creation speaking those words that brought to being all that is. That creation is now perfected when Christ speaks the words that destroy the evil that has perverted creation.

At his arrest in the garden, Jesus told his disciples not to resist with the sword and ended his command by saying, "Do you think I cannot call on my Father, and he will at once put at my disposal more than twelve legions of angels?" (Matthew 26:53). Jesus then went, filled with faith, to the patient endurance of a bitter death. Now the time has come for those legions; and as King of kings, Christ gathers the "armies of heaven" (19:14) and goes to do war with evil.

❑ *Revelation 19:17-21.* The actual battle between Christ and the forces of evil is not narrated. It need not be. In a single word Satan is defeated.

The grisly scene of birds feeding on the corpses of horses and riders slain by the sword of his mouth is, indeed, difficult to deal with. (See Ezekiel 39:17-20.) Evil is ugly, and the results of evil are even uglier. We lie when we color evil any other color than hideous.

The capture and restraint of the two beasts (the false Christ and the false prophet) bring to a temporary end their mission of deceit. In the next scene the source of deceit, Satan, will also be temporarily chained.

"The fiery lake of burning sulfur" will be a frequent image in Chapter 20. Since water quenches fire, sulfur (or brimstone) is added to the solution to convey a sense of how water could burn. The meaning of this torture is rich and deep.

❑ *Revelation 20:1-3.* Revelation is so artistically written that the reader is tempted to heave a great sigh of relief when Satan is chained up. But his imprisonment is not a permanent reprieve for the world. Satan is imprisoned for only a thousand years—a millennium. This idea is based on certain portions of the Creation story. The perfect creation of God was corrupted by sin. Because the creation is God's gift to the world, it must be restored. Therefore, an event and a time need to be established for this restoration. The chaining of Satan is the first event that signals the restoration of God's creation.

In a sense, then, this millennium is a time for the earth in all its parts to enjoy life as it was meant to be in the paradise of Eden. The earth and the faithful people of God need this period to prepare for the "new heaven and ... new earth" (21:1) that will have no end.

❑ *Revelation 20:4-6.* John's description of this millennial respite is actually quite brief. He does not dwell on what life is like for those who have remained faithful. He only projects a limited resurrection of the martyrs. (He calls this "the first resurrection," suggesting that the resurrection of all human beings who have died previously will wait for the final resurrection [20:13].) The only detail of description John offers is that the Christian martyrs are "priests" (20:6) who will "reign" with Christ and God (20:4cd, 6b).

Yet, this description tells us a great deal. The martyrs are in Christ's presence. The greatest honor, thus, is not mere physical existence without the threat of pain, disease, and death but the enjoyment of Christ's company. In this life of continual fellowship, the martyrs are priests. We usually think of a priest as someone who celebrates the presence of Christ in the Lord's Supper. In the millennial period of restoration, however, there will be no need for Holy Communion. Christ will be continually present. Why, then, do they need a company of priests (1:6; 5:10)? Priests are those who live in the midst of praise and celebration of God, calling all creation to join in songs of rejoicing and praise.

❑ *Revelation 20:7-10.* In the remainder of this chapter, John sketches with quick strokes the events that bring to a close life as it has been known since the dawn of creation. The idea of Gog and Magog gathering vast armies to make war on the righteous is taken directly from Ezekiel 38.

The final defeat of Satan is really no battle at all. The armies raised by Satan following his release are simply destroyed by fire from heaven. When these armies are destroyed, Satan is defeated forever. The false Christ and false prophet wait for their leader in "the lake of burning sulfur" (20:10). Into this inferno of eternal torment Satan is cast, to "be tormented for ever and ever."

❑ *Revelation 20:11-15.* All parts of the New Testament reflect a belief in a judgment at the conclusion of the present age. In Revelation this judgment depends on the universal resurrection of the earth's dead. The living have been judged, but now attention turns to the dead. The visual image of this judgment requires a written record that contains the biography of the lives of all who have lived and died in the world's history. A slightly different idea has already been reviewed in 13:8. There, John referred to a "book of life" that contains only the names of those who are to be granted salvation. This "book of life" reappears here ("The dead were judged according to what they had done as recorded in the books" [20:12].). John's vision, then, includes several books: a "book of life" containing the names of the saved and possibly a set of books containing the records of every person's life.

More difficult, however, is the repeated phrase "what they had done" (20:12c, 13). "What they had done" here likely means deeds of faith in which commitment and fidelity to the Christ who brought salvation is the premium deed that overshadows all others.

In contrast, commitment of one's life and energies to the many false gods and prophets is the deed of damnation. Those who have lived by the dictates of Satan and his servants will share the fellowship of their disappointing lord. If the apex of paradise is the enjoyment of Christ's unceasing presence, the essence of eternal punishment is the constant presence of Satan.

DIMENSION THREE:
WHAT DOES THE BIBLE MEAN TO ME?

Revelation 19:1-10

When was the last time you could hardly keep from saying aloud, "Hallelujah! For the Lord our God Almighty reigns"? One of the remarkable facts about Revelation is that John filled it with words of beautiful poetry and praise directed in joy to God. This fact is remarkable simply because we know that John and those to whom he wrote were suffering under oppression and daily threat of death. Think of examples of persons you know or have read or heard about who illustrate this kind of living.

Revelation 19:11-16

Persons who are concerned about issues of war and peace may be disturbed by the portrayal of Christ as a victorious warrior. In what way is the militarism of this passage different from our own? In this passage Christ "makes war" (19:11), even as God does on occasion in the Old Testament. How can this image be reconciled with our identity as peacemakers?

THE SWORD OF HIS MOUTH

Revelation 19:17-21

The beast and the false prophet are familiar to us. Can you imagine how they are able to trick the nations of the world into going to battle with Christ? Use your imagination. Try to re-create in your mind the arguments used today in the councils of politicians who encourage aggressive acts. What kind of emotions are triggered? What part does misinformation play? Why do some people always want to believe the worst about others, rather than the best?

Revelation 20:1-10

Many people find the description of this "heaven on earth" appealing. How do you feel about this description? What do you think life would be like today if evil were not present and the living Christ were? What would you wish for the world and for yourself if suspicion, envy, self-centeredness, and deceit were no longer facts of existence? In many ways the teachings of Christ in the Gospels describe such a world. What keeps you from acting for the common good of your neighbor now?

Revelation 20:11-15

What are your feelings about the claim made in 20:15 that those whose name is "not found written in the book of life" will be punished? Notice that only God can make such a judgment. Should we judge other persons? How does the idea of God committing people to a "lake of fire" fit with our understanding of a God of love?

*I am the Alpha and the Omega, the Beginning and
the End (21:6b).*

— 12 —
I Make All Things New
Revelation 21

**DIMENSION ONE:
WHAT DOES THE BIBLE SAY?**

Answer these questions by reading Revelation 21

1. What happens to our heaven and earth in John's final
   vision? (21:1)

2. What does John see "coming down out of heaven from
   God"? (21:2)

3. What image does John use to describe "the new Jerusalem"? (21:2)

4. Who first speaks to John in his vision? (21:3)

5. What is the message from the "loud voice"? (21:3-4)

6. Who speaks next? (21:5a)

7. What does God command John to do? (21:5b)

8. What is the message John is to write down? (21:6-8)

9. Who appears next in John's vision? (21:9)

10. What does this angel want with John? (21:9)

11. What does John see from the "mountain great and high"? (21:10-11)

12. How does John describe the Holy City? (21:12-14)

13. What does the angel do next? (21:15)

14. What description comes from this measurement? (21:16-17)

15. What is the city made of? (21:18-21)

16. Is there a temple in the city? What form does it take? (21:22)

17. What else is missing, and why? (21:23-24)

18. Who is drawn into the city by its light? (21:24, 26)

19. Is the city open? (21:25)

20. Who can and who cannot enter the city? (21:27)

DIMENSION TWO:
WHAT DOES THE BIBLE MEAN?

❑ *Revelation 21:1-4.* The opening lines of this chapter make clear that the issue is no longer one of restoration of what was. Revelation 20:1-6 presents a different perspective. There, evil is chained and Eden restored. In Revelation 21, John sees an entirely new reality: "A new heaven and a new earth." The most difficult question—and one that has troubled readers for centuries—is whether this new creation is a reality happening at the same time as human history. Or is this new creation a distant, future reality to be realized only when human history ends in tragic conflagration?

Those persons who are discontent and cynical about the possibilities of God's redeeming power in the present will strongly encourage us to accept the second option as the only reasonable view. However, much in this chapter encourages us to believe that the city of God is an ever-present reality in all ages and times. Of course, the words of Revelation 21:1 seem to speak of a change in the nature of things. But this change is reflected in the prophet's present vision. Throughout this chapter John speaks of the city as a present reality that draws all peoples and their leaders to it. Finally, we only have to consider the effect of relegating the hopes of this chapter to a far-distant future beyond history to reject such an unnecessary limitation.

The city of God is a gift from God, not the result of human labor and ingenuity. This message comes from the words of the text and from the tone of the text. The voice speaking from the throne of God speaks for God in vivid colors of covenant language. God will dwell with humans, and they will be God's people. These words are the familiar words of the covenant God made with Abraham and Moses (Genesis 17:2-8; Exodus 2:24; 6:2-4; 34:10-28).

These words are only the beginning of the means by which John seeks to unify all human history in the metaphor of the city. The result of the covenant is the redemption of all that seeks to defeat and destroy the bonding of the divine-human encounter—sorrow, pain, suffering, and death. The difference is that the realization of this salvation is presented as a reality and no mere hope.

This vision of the city of God, therefore, is incomplete. The completeness of fulfillment is yet to be realized. How is the vision incomplete and also complete? To the extent that pain and sorrow, much less death, have not been erased from human experience, the city of God is still a vision to be realized by means of divine intervention. But tears are wiped away;

mourning has an end; and pain passes, if only quieted by death. As we shall see in the next passage, the gift of life is a present reality that persists into the unknown.

The major means of further identifying this city is by the image of a bride. The Gospels of Matthew, Mark, and Luke speak often of the bridegroom (Matthew 9:15; 25:1-13; Mark 2:19-20; Luke 5:34-35). Only the Gospel of John and Revelation also use the idea of bride, and only Revelation develops this image fully (19:7; 22:17).

How is the city of God also a bride? When we read ahead in this chapter, a rather clear picture emerges. The city of God is the fullness of God's people found in all times and places—past, present, and future. They are a people—a city—not made with hands, but created by the divine initiative of grace. They live only by the presence of God in their midst. This city is not made; it is given. The means by which the city was created is seen in the redeeming acts of God in history: the covenant at Sinai; the words of the prophets; but most clearly and supremely, the gift of God's Son. For this reason Christ is presented as the Bridegroom who claims as his bride a people.

❑ *Revelation 21:5-8.* John often refers to God as Creator. This chapter captures that dominant theme. When God speaks in the first person from the throne, the identity claimed is that of one who creates: "I am making everything new!" (21:5). Much as at the conclusion of Creation (Genesis 1:31), here God declares his creation of redemption complete: "It is done!" (21:6).

Still speaking in the first person, God reveals a divine name: "I am the Alpha and the Omega, the Beginning and the End" (21:6). Reflect on this phrase as a name for God. John begins Revelation with this name as an identification of God (1:8) and concludes in the same way (22:13). What does it mean for God to be defined as the beginning and ending of all things? To paraphrase what is meant by Alpha and Omega, God is the cause of existence and also the final word in the destiny of existence. The process of life's journey between these two points is most intriguing. By reflecting on God as Omega, humans assume that life is actually going somewhere. The struggle, however, lies between Alpha and Omega. Here the metaphor of the Holy City can apply its healing vision.

God declares, "To him who is thirsty I will give to drink without cost from the spring of the water of life" (21:6c). The gift of life is by means of God's free gift of grace. This affirmation overshadows any temptation to see the quest for the city of God as a romantic adventure under the control of human courage and inspiration.

This dependence on God's grace is balanced by yet another use of vivid covenant language. We are made children of God by means of entering into covenant with God. But this covenant carries with it obligations on our side. Our responsibility is to "overcome" (21:7). From earlier encounters with this idea in Revelation (2:7b, 11b, 17b, 26; 3:5, 12, 21), we know that *overcome* is a summarizing concept that means the responsibility to resist evil in all its forms. We have learned in Revelation that conquering is made doubly difficult by the ingenious and subtle nature of evil. The major tool of Satan is deceit, the artful disguising of evil as good. Thus the task is to know evil and resist it. Often the most difficult part of this twin task is the first.

Recognizing evil, John says, is a tricky business because of a particular human trait: Human beings tend to elevate that which they have created to a level of idolatry. The most dangerous evil is the one we have deified as good. We do not recognize as dangerous that which is closest to our heart. For this reason we dare not identify the city of God as identical with our church or any church, much less deify our conclusions about God.

❑ *Revelation 21:9-14.* The most remarkable aspect of the Holy City's description is that only the walls, gates, and foundation are identified. Essentially, the city is empty. This description is not an accident, nor is it sloppy writing. If the city is God's people, then the city is populated by all those persons who seek the new Jerusalem.

All the faithful, including those of Israel, are included in the city's structures. At the first throne room vision (4:4), we discovered twenty-four elders where we might have expected twelve. The reason may be that John is anxious to include

God's creation of Israel in his vision of salvation. John accomplishes that inclusion here by naming the twelve gates after the twelve tribes of Israel and the twelve foundations for the twelve apostles.

We also might recall that the 144,000 redeemed is a mathematical metaphor for the unity of God's people—including those whom God called by covenanting with Israel. This aspect of Revelation we dare not miss; for it saves the book from a narrow, sectarian view that neglects the scope of salvation history. We are a people with a past. That past is brought into a comprehensive unity by many means in Revelation. This fact only serves to emphasize the importance of Revelation in Scripture.

❑ *Revelation 21:15-21.* John most likely did not think of this city as a physical city placed in time and space. Rather, the city is an idea whose power exceeds the potential of geography and architecture.

The city is mathematical perfection, a symbol of the city's representative unity. As a perfect cube, the city is enormous. Probably John did not intend the numbers to be taken literally; his intention was to present a city not existing in space and time and, therefore, limitless in scope. This meaning is hinted at by the cryptic clause "by man's measurement, which the angel was using" (21:17). In other words, we do not even know what a cubit translates to in God's terms. Further, the figure of 144 cubits reminds us of the 144,000 saints mentioned frequently in Revelation. In that case the symbol is a mathematical metaphor for the fullness of the number 12. The same is true of the "12,000 stadia" (21:16), another multiple of 12.

❑ *Revelation 21:22-27.* If we have any doubt that John does not envision a physical, reconstructed temple in time and space, this passage puts that doubt to rest. The city of God is populated by the people of God who worship and glorify God and the Lamb. This theme is linked with the tradition found in all the Gospels in which Jesus declares the end of the Temple in Jerusalem. Jesus symbolically made his declaration by cleansing the Temple and by saying that the Jerusalem temple would soon be destroyed. The point of Jesus' encounter in the Temple is not that worship in the Temple needs to be restored to some previous state of purity but that he has come to take the place of the Temple.

John's point here, that the Lamb is the Temple, is therefore quite consistent with the Gospels. This insight is a gateway to understandings that are virtually limitless in their possibilities. For example, if the Lamb and God are the temple for the people of God, then worship in the temple consists of all encounters with the divine presence. Worship is no longer limited to the forms normally accepted. If one finds God in the service of the poor, outcast, and suffering, then one lives and works in the temple of God.

The point of the presence of God and the Lamb is the light they bring to the city. As Matthew reports the words of Jesus, "A city on a hill cannot be hidden" (Matthew 5:14b). Such a city cannot be hidden because of its light, which is the point of the Holy City's light. In a surprising turn John says that the objective of this eternally lighted city is its drawing power for the people of the world.

The city exists to glorify God and point the way for all peoples. The city's purpose is to evangelize. A remarkable mood of invitation is cast by the description of the gates: "On no day will its gates ever be shut" (21:25). The nations of all times and places are invited to bring their limited glory to the limitless glory of God's light. This statement is the redeeming, final grace note of Revelation. The door is not shut. Jerusalem and Rome may be in ashes at different times, but the kings and peoples of the earth need not mourn for these great cities. The city of God stands eternal with the light of God's love shining brightly.

DIMENSION THREE:
WHAT DOES THE BIBLE MEAN TO ME?

Revelation 21:1-4

In this chapter we find ourselves captivated by a fresh, new vision that offers hope, not only for the future but also for the present. The word *new* springs out to greet us. We are meant to feel our spirits rise when we come to this heavenly vision of a new heaven and a new earth. What does the word *new* mean to you? What have you learned to look forward to with great expectancy in your life? Does the hope of a new beginning create inspiration in your mind when you think about it?

The great hope associated with *new* in this chapter is, of course, the greatest *new* that can ever be contemplated. The newness described in this chapter relates to all of life. If we welcome a new season, a new friend, a new job, a new time in our life, then we have an idea of the possibilities in this *new*. Do you think of new things as cause for joy? Or do you find the new unwelcome, something to be feared?

As John presents the new heaven and new earth in this chapter, they are, above all, a profound gift from God. Responding to this gift from God is the challenge that calls us into a newness of life. As the chapter proceeds, John takes care to point out that the possibilities presented by this heavenly city are limitless. Do you respond to this message with hope, or do you find it so strange and otherworldly as to lack credibility?

Revelation 21:5-14

John presents God as calling God's people into a covenant relationship. The people of God find in this relationship the fulfillment of all their needs. The text of Revelation 21, often used in the Christian service of burial, envisions the possibility of release from grief, suffering, pain, and even death. When you read these words about the redemption promised to God's people, do you respond with a sense of affirmation? Can we believe so completely in the gift of life that fear of death becomes inconsequential? Someone has said that most of us spend all our lives preparing to confront the most difficult part of life, death. What do you think about this statement? When you think about your own death, what meaning can you attach to it? Do you think God is able to wipe away tears, suffering, and grief? If so, do you think this act will take place only in the future? Or do you think that in some sense God gives us release and comfort in the present moment?

Revelation 21:15-21

The idea of measuring is a metaphor. When we measure something, we take account of it. Measuring creates the possibility of comprehending a person or place. As the temple is described and measured, we begin to understand that this city cannot be fixed anywhere in time and space. This vision of completeness makes possible the redemption of the present. This vision, of course, does not rob the present of its future potential but only increases the sense of realization on our part that we are called in the here-and-now to walk these streets of gold. What part of the city's description have you found most interesting? What have you found most troubling? What do you think is the main point of the extravagance with which the city is built? Every part of the city is precious in some sense. What do you think this wealth is meant to convey?

Revelation 21:22-27

John ends his vision by returning to the call to be engaged in a mission of proclamation. What do you think the responsibility of all of us as Christians is in this mission? As John presents "the Holy City," it creates a light that attracts the kings and nations of earth to the city. To what extent does this light shine only through us? If the light is God and Christ, how can we be the light? We have also said that the great light of this city cannot be completely and totally identified with any earthly reality, including the church. Do you agree with this statement? To what extent is the church, as you know and understand it, the same thing as the city of God? Do you think that this Holy City has the possibility of attracting the kings of earth today? Can you think of any modern examples in which the city of God has drawn others to it? Finally, do you think that this chapter contains the possibility of shedding light on our life today? Or is this chapter simply a description of a myth that is limited in its power to help people escape from the hopelessness of real earthly existence?

*Blessed is he who keeps the words of the prophecy
in this book (22:7b).*

— 13 —

The Healing Stream

Revelation 22

DIMENSION ONE:
WHAT DOES THE BIBLE SAY?

Answer these questions by reading Revelation 22

1. What is the source of the remarkable river shown to John in the vision? (22:1)

2. What is this river's course? (22:2a)

3. What is remarkable about the tree of life? (22:2bc)

4. How does John describe the city of God? (22:3)

5. What are the two privileges given to those who dwell in the city of God? (22:4)

6. What has God done for his servants? (22:6b)

7. According to the message given to the prophet John, what event is foretold? (22:7a)

8. Who is given a special blessing? (22:7b)

9. By what name does the author of Revelation identify himself? (22:8a)

10. The angel warns John not to do what? (22:10)

11. Who is to remain in the same condition in light of the nearness of time? (22:11)

12. What will Christ and God do when this happens? (22:12)

13. Who is blessed, and what do they receive? (22:14)

14. Who must live outside the gates of the city of God? (22:15)

15. How does Jesus describe the book that John has written? (22:16a)

16. By what names does Jesus identify himself? (22:16b)

17. Why are all persons who are thirsty invited to "come"? (22:17)

18. What are the warnings given to all who might want to change the words of Revelation? (22:18-19)

19. Who is it that witnesses to the words of Revelation, and what does he say? (22:20a)

20. How does John respond to these words of Jesus? (22:20bc)

DIMENSION TWO:
WHAT DOES THE BIBLE MEAN?

❏ *Revelation 22:1-5.* We have been waiting since 21:6 to discover the source of "the spring of the water of life." Now John describes this source. The source of this water is the throne we have so often encountered in Revelation (4:2-11; 5:1-13; 7:9-17). We should not pass this detail by too quickly, since this idea is so predominant in Revelation. The throne itself, of course, is not the point. Rather, the idea of sovereign authority

THE HEALING STREAM   **103** as symbolized by the figure of the throne excites the imagination.

The action of Revelation frequently returns to find its reference point in the throne room scenes sprinkled throughout the book. This action is both an artistic literary arrangement and a theological statement. Viewed from a purely aesthetic perspective, the visions of judgment, deceit, and death that predominate in so much of Revelation would be too chaotic to bear, or be credible, if they were linked up one upon the other. But they are not. Rather, John punctuates these horrific visions by rhythmic returns to the vision of worship before God's throne. We capture there, by the miracle of narrative, a sense of the stability that makes possible the contemplation of evil and its judgment. The saints need not be terrified by the unmasking of evil because God is in control of the outcome. Or, better said, the Christian need not be afraid to confront evil and tear from it the mask of deceit because God is the source of evil's distortion.

We have been constantly reminded that God is the source of the just judgment against evil, but now we are also reminded that God is the source of life. And the word *source* here is used as a kind of religious or moral geographical term. Because the city of God does not belong exclusively to any particular space or time, we can also say that God is in all times and places the source of living water.

This image has a long and remarkable history. The garden of Eden, part of God's first creation, had a river and a tree of life (Genesis 2:8-10; 3:22). Ezekiel, one of John's favorite Old Testament prophets, elaborated on this image in a similar, but more detailed, description of the river and trees (Ezekiel 47:1-12). In Ezekiel the river flows from a new temple. This river has been transformed by John into a timeless river flowing in the midst of a holy city without geographic boundary.

While John speaks of a singular idea ("tree" of life), Ezekiel's vision evidently has deeply penetrated John's thinking; for the word picture is clearly of a river lined with many trees. In fact, we are encouraged to think of this image as a lush display of foliage and fruit. The exact point, by the way, of everbearing fruit is not clear. (The point in Ezekiel 47:12 is that the trees feed people, and this meaning is possibly also the idea here.)

The leaves of these trees contain the healing properties. In Ezekiel's vision the leaves were used as poultices for healing physical problems. However, John goes further. As we saw in 21:24-26, the real purpose of the city of God is to enlighten the nations. Now we learn that the healing leaves of these life-giving trees are for the same purpose.

One could hardly imagine a beauty that could surpass that of "the new Jerusalem." But this, of course, is a metaphor for the true beauty found only when one enters the Holy City. As John conveys it, this is the beauty of holiness. And "holiness" is beautiful because it finds its true center in the source of all holiness. This is why the only activity in the city of God is worship.

As we have seen, worship in Revelation is the placing of God in the right role—that of sovereign Lord of creation and history. When God is in the right role, all the rest of existence falls into place. Thus we could say that the healing of the nations takes place when the human cities of the nations are gathered into the city of God. Care should be taken not to limit this healing only to a distant hope beyond history. We are also called in the present to seek the enlightenment and healing of the cities.

Seeing the face of God is a frequent allusion in both the Old and New Testaments. In general the face of God is a metaphor conveying the sense of ultimate privilege, since seeing another's face is the best means of revelation. To see God's face would mean to know God as fully as humanly possible. This, combined with the reference to continual worship in the Holy City, makes good sense of the notion that the purpose of life is to know and enjoy God forever.

In Revelation 3:12, the martyrs were marked with God's name. This notion of identity is repeated here.

❑ *Revelation 22:6-7a.* Revelation 22 contains extensive repetition of Revelation 21. The declaration that the words of the prophecy are "trustworthy and true" (22:6) is an excellent example (21:5b). But here the assurance that these words are reliable and sound is used to support a new idea. While hearers of Revelation may not doubt that the words spoken by the risen Christ are "trustworthy and true," they may well have doubted that the prophet John's words were really the words of Christ. This is the classic problem of prophecy. While we are much more skeptical (and rightly so!) when a modern "prophet" says that God is speaking through his or her mouth, it is still true that prophets have always been regarded with skepticism.

In the history of the classical prophecy of the Hebrew Scriptures, we even find examples of two prophets delivering messages from God that do not agree. Perhaps the best-known case is that of Jeremiah and Hananiah. The story is narrated in Jeremiah 27 and 28. There, Jeremiah appears in the Temple precincts wearing a yoke and repeating that God has commanded him to proclaim a message symbolized by the yoke. The message is that God is going to permit Nebuchadnezzar and the Babylonians to defeat and take Judah into exile, but eventually God will break the yoke of Babylon and return Judah to the land of Israel. This message, of course, was hard for Judah to hear. Jeremiah, knowing that the bad news was not going to be received with pleasure, concluded his message from God with these words: "Do not listen to the words of the prophets who say . . ." (Jeremiah 27:16). Remarkably, one prophet advises against listening to another; yet both claim to speak for God.

Little wonder, then, that near the conclusion of his prophetic report, John quotes a special message given him by his angel-guide: "The Lord, the God of the spirits of the prophets, sent his angel to show his servants the things that must soon take place" (22:6b). Since it is by the Spirit that prophecy takes place (1:10 and frequently throughout Revelation), the reassurance given here is that it is God who has been in control of the prophet's spirit, not an alien force.

A more complex question concerns the words of assurance spoken, we are to assume, directly by Christ: "I am coming soon" (22:7a). That these words are to be taken as a comforting reassurance to those Christians living under oppression is clear. But are they also in some sense an affirmation of the prophet's truthful account of his vision? If so, the connection between the two points might be that the nearness of the return of Christ is, itself, an assurance that John's words are to be heeded.

How does this follow logically? Only the event itself can prove or disprove the prior word of the prophet. To return to Jeremiah, listen to his conclusion of the conflict between himself and Hananiah, who prophesied that peace would reign between Judah and Babylon: "But the prophet who prophesies peace will be recognized as one truly sent by the LORD only if his prediction comes true" (Jeremiah 28:9).

In the case of Jeremiah, peace did not come to pass; and he was proved thereby to be the true prophet—even though his human sense of compassion found him praying aloud that it be he that be proved wrong rather than Hananiah! But, in the case of John, Jesus did not soon return—a fact that must be faced and dealt with if Revelation and, indeed, orthodox Christianity are to keep their integrity.

❏ *Revelation 22:7b.* "Blessed is he who keeps the words of the prophecy in this book." The call to keep the teachings of this book is persistent in Revelation (1:3; 14:12). So much is this the case as to raise the question, Why must this call be repeated? Is it not clear what is at stake for the person who neglects these teachings? Actually, the specific command-ments are not easily distilled into a precise list such as that found in the Sermon on the Mount. In fact, the call to "keep the words" is quite general. Above all, the faithful hearer "keeps" this book by seeing more clearly the full dimension of reality.

Revelation includes an almost aesthetic vocation; and per-haps this is why Revelation has, throughout the centuries, appealed especially to artists, musicians, and mystics. The aesthetics of Revelation are, however, not those of an art for art's sake mentality but those of enhanced perception for the sake of truth and understanding. Above all, Revelation teaches the lesson of careful observation and cogent analysis. This may explain why Revelation has often been used as a textbook for oppressed peoples.

❏ *Revelation 22:8-11.* The mood of John's first-person report in this section returns us to the inaugural vision (beginning in 1:9). For the first time in many pages, we hear directly the words of the prophet. As in 19:10, John's response to the conclusion of his vision is to worship the angel-guide. Again, he is told to worship God.

❑ *Revelation 22:10-11.* We may have thought this would be the end of the book, but a kind of mini-epilogue continues. While some of the themes of this epilogue repeat those found in Revelation 21 and elsewhere, John includes much that is new and rich here.

The command not to "seal up" (that is, the command not to reveal what has been written by John) is not at all strange. We may assume that a book is written to be read—especially one that was written to reveal. However, this kind of literature was often kept secret. Paul chose not to reveal what was revealed to him in his extraordinary spiritual visit to the "third heaven" (2 Corinthians 12:2-4). Daniel was commanded by his angel to "go your way . . . because the words are closed up and sealed until the time of the end" (Daniel 12:9). In fact, John was also commanded to suppress some of what he heard, such as when the seven thunders spoke (Revelation 10:4). Overall, however, Revelation is differentiated from much of the rest of apocalyptic literature by its nonsecretive nature. This is a true irony in the light of the subsequent history of interpretation; for many have tired to turn Revelation into a "sealed" book, to which only *they* have the key.

The exhortation of 22:11 is simply a poetic way of saying that the interval between the writing of Revelation and the return of Christ is so short as to eliminate the possibility of change. This statement is a good example of prophetic license in the form of hyperbole. Clearly John would never intend to suggest that repentance is ever too late.

❑ *Revelation 22:12-13.* Nothing original is found in these verses. All that is said here is said elsewhere. (See Revelation 21:5-8.)

❑ *Revelation 22:14-15.* This blessing is the seventh blessing offered in Revelation. (The others are found in 1:3; 14:13; 16:15; 19:9; 20:6; 22:7b.) Both the Lamb and the martyrs appear consistently in Revelation in robes of white, dipped in the blood of Christ's crucifixion (7:9, 13, 14; 19:13). The white robes are a symbol of redemption.

The access to the entire city and, specifically, the tree(s) of life appears here as a reward for those who have received the gift of redemption wrought through the death of Christ. Later, in verse 17, access to the water that nourishes the trees of life will be included. The list of those excluded from the city of God is quite similar to that in Revelation 21:8.

❏ *Revelation 22:16.* This verse draws the circle of Revelation to a close. In 1:11, John was told, "Write on a scroll what you see and send it to the seven churches." The source of prophecy is the risen Christ, and it has been he who has directed the interaction of the angel with John.

❏ *Revelation 22:17-19.* John now speaks—first for the Spirit that has inspired his vision, then for the entire people of God, then for himself. The closing words of Revelation are, appropriately, an invitation to life. This should give us pause in light of the way Revelation has frequently been presented—as a book of death. The warnings presented by John are unusual but are not unknown in Scripture (Deuteronomy 4:2; 12:32). Perhaps John sensed that his prophesy would be subject to abuse and misunderstanding.

❏ *Revelation 22:20-21.* While John understands that he is only the mouthpiece of the risen Christ, nevertheless the words of John spoken here seem to echo a kind of solemn antiquity. At the time of writing Revelation, Jesus had been gone from earth at least sixty years. So immediate is the sense of Christ's presence in this book, however, that the reader knows right away that it is Jesus Christ who says, "I am coming soon" (22:20). This statement is not new in Revelation, but it is a powerful way to conclude.

The final words before the "grace" wish of verse 21 are a spontaneous outburst of the prophet himself. Through the remarkable gift of the spirit of prophecy, John not only hears Jesus speak but also hears himself respond. When John says, "Amen," he is stating his affirmation of Christ's promise to return soon. When he says, "Come, Lord Jesus," he is using one of the earliest of Christian prayers. By reading, discussing, and reflecting on the message of Revelation, we have joined with the prophet John in saying, "Come, Lord Jesus!"

DIMENSION THREE:
WHAT DOES THE BIBLE MEAN TO ME?

As you reflect on the course of your study of Revelation, what are the most significant values that have been left with you?

In this final chapter we come very close to the experience of Moses when he nearly saw God "face to face." Revelation 22 holds out the potential for such final lifting of the barriers surrounding our full enjoyment of the divine. What is it, do you think, that stands most in our way, preventing us from "seeing God face to face"?

What are we to make of the sense of urgency in Revelation? What are the conditions and circumstances that might lead to such a dominating sense of urgency? Is there any sense in which the world's agenda is urgent? Do you think the condition of the world is more urgent than at earlier times in history? Why does every generation feel a sense of urgency?

Finally, this chapter has a great message of healing. Use your imagination. What needs healing most in our world? in your neighborhood? in your life and those of your family members? Do you think that the healing of the nations spoken of in this chapter offers any hope for the world today? As John presents his vision of healing and expectation, what is it that most captivates your imagination? Do you think Revelation 22 has a message for you?